mend my dress

collected zines
2005-2007

by Neely Bat Chestnut

MEND MY DRESS
Collected Zines: 2005-2007
Neely Bat Chestnut

© 2012 by Neely Bat Chestnut

Cover art by Mend My Dress Press

Published by Mend My Dress Press, Tacoma, WA
MendMyDress@gmail.com, MendMyDress.com

Library of Congress Cataloging-in-Publication Data

Chestnut, Neely Bat
  Mend My Dress : Collected Zines / Neely Bat Chestnut
  Edited by Colleen Weber Borst
  p. cm
  ISBN-13 978-0-9850131-0-3 (pb)
  1. Zines. 2. Feminism. 3. Women's studies. 4. Autobiography
  I. Title

                            2012931628

Manufactured in the United States of America

Contents

Months ago, i was turning over
thoughts about mend my dress in
my head. trying to decide if i
should continue to make copies.
unsure if anyone wanted them
anymore. did they matter. later
that day i receved an email from
a lady. she wanted to buy back
issues for a zine library she was
working for. i pulled out my huge
folder of originals and flats,
found some copies to put together
for her.

Looking over those pages i felt
horrible. my heart floating some-
where xabove everything. like
nothing had changed and i no
longer was my body. the same
feeling i used to get while in a
room with my family. reading the
bits of text i felt silly, ashamed
at all the mistakes. Misspellings
and wrong words. Overlooking those
i am still taken aback at how much
i have changed. after writing that
last issue, i have bought a house
adopted two pet rabbits, legaly
changed my name and i no longer
speak to my father.

Re-reading these zines i
can not help but cringe.

thanking internet
friends i have long sence lost
all contact with, thanking an
ex-boyfriend that turned out
to be an abusive prick. I am
also taken back to the

begining of the healing
process.

Writing mend my dress was the great catalyst
for healing. at years old they tell the
   story of how i felt, rather than how i feel.
these thoughts exist in a time i no longer
   care to visit over the photocopy machine
   every once and awhile. of course i could
   just stop. let these words die, but i
know they are too important for that.

     I know too well the frustration with other
writers that let their work go out of print.
i often want all the issues of some great

new zine i have only now just heard of.

          here i give you a middle ground.
   all of my old zines safe together in their
   very own book. As i contune to create more
zines, me and these pages will drift even
furtur   further apart. they are still dear
to me. please enjoy.
                        xoxlove- neelybat

*notes-
   Grit and Glitter was a split between

   Hazel Pine and I. She gets all
          credit for layout.

mend my dress

"Oh dear," said Cinderella.

"I will never have time

to mend my dress."

when i was younger, i was raped/molested by my father. when i was
twelve or so me and my step brother ~~had an affair~~ he was a few years
older than me. when i was sixteen i got into an abusive relationship
with a boy that lasted around four years. i am trying to move on and
i am reading the book the courage to heal. in the book they tell you
to write about the abuse and things related to it. the part of the
book that helps me the most is hearing other peoples stories. so i
thought, maybe i should just put all of my writings together in a
zine format, maybe it will help someone else along the way. maybe
someone will understand and maybe some one else will take on the
challenge of healing. if anything, it will help me by writing it all
out and making copies. I'm tired of holding these secrets in.
write me, neely_ohara@hellokitty.com

a list of things i like.
[glitter.] $1.25 tofu sandwiches from down the block, light shining
through leaves, zine libraries, playing records all day alone,
writing in livejournal, reading history books,
(book, movie, soundtrack, score, web site),
heavens to betsy, pressed flowers,
growing flowers, the virgin suicides
        knee socks, sock garters,
    singing to myself, moss, insects,
    imaging perfect friendships,

            owning things that once
        belonged to people that are now dead.
    holding hands with anyone that will let me,
                    fairy tales,
    maryjane shoes. music from far away places.

the sun is still in the sky.

Maybe this is timed.wrong. Maybe i should have written this when i was 15, 16. maybe i will not get as much credit because of my age. maybe this is not exciting because I'm not in high school anymore. maybe i should be over this; i should just be on friendly terms with my emotions, my father, my mother. maybe I'm too old for this, but I'm still the six year old girl who fakes a tummy ache every time it's time for the spelling tests at school, and I'm the same scared little girl hoping dad will fall asleep before me tonight every time i hear his voice.

i am in second grade. i have just finished my spelling lessons. the house is dark and smoky. my father smokes a lot. he has always smoked the cheapest brand cigarettes he can buy. smokes other things from a pipe that smell better and drinks. drinks huge glasses of wine from the cheap jug. i don't remember ever being young and noticing.he drunk, or stoned, but I'm sure he was. we fished my home work, i did ok, better than last week, but still not very well. spelling has always been hard for me, when writing i will reword a whole line of script just to hide form a hard word. see, i just did. it's time for bed. i don't remember if i brushed my teeth or not. we went to sleep in his queen sized bed. my father never thought to ask if i wanted my own bed, and i didn't think it was my place to ask. maybe i just didn't know to ask. the sheets are mismatched, one white, the other a strange yellow/ orange mix.

my pillow case is jungle animals, monkeys and birds with huge beaks. the lions are green and the tigers are purple. it's some 1970's nightmare of the forest being fucked in the ass of the yellow submarine all over my pillow. i got to sleep with my tank top, a white one with little purple flowers all over it, i have a long sleeved shirt over it. underwear, and i think a pair of shorts, maybe a shirt. i push myself in to the corner, and fall asleep. i wake up later, maybe it's early morning. there was some light, but very little. just enough to see the horrible scene on my pillow case. i am pushed up against his chest and my back is sweating and my chest is sweating and i try to wriggle out but he is snoring and his arms are heavy and the harder is try the more panicked i get, and the more scared i am the more awake i am the more i notice what i am not wearing. all of my clothing is gone, stuffed in the spot between the mattress and the wall. somehow i manage to get out from under my fathers heavy arms. put my clothes back on, and never mention it to him. later at school, i tell my best friend Sarah, about the weird thing that happened. Sarah, with the huge white house on the beach and the pilot father and the house wife mother and all the brothers and sisters and the new kids on the block room. Sarah with the brown hair and the family in Italy and all the money. Sarah with every Disney movie on video and the best lunches. i tell her about the weird morning and how i am scared of my dad and i don't know what happened. she promises not to ever tell anyone. She pinky swears that she will not tell on me. she is my best friend. At lunch that day i am sitting with another friend, (now i don't remember who it was) Sarah walks up with another girl, a girl i am not friends with and they ask, laughing, "hey, did you really wake up in bed with your dad, naked!?!

Cinderella

bravely

started

to walk

the plank.

"You must learn to work faster," said the stepmother.

Ewww.....ahahahahahaha! "i lied, "no." and they made fun of me and called me a liar and told everyone i was to poor to have my own bed and that i was gross because i wanted to sleep with my dad. i know the teachers must of heard what they where saying, because one of them told the girls to be quite. but no teachers ever asked me why i was crying and didn't have those friends at lunch; no one asked me why i just sat in the library. i never ever wanted to tell anyone ever again. if you can't trust your best friend, or your father, who can you trust. i never wanted anyone to know. i never wanted to explain myself to anyone; i didn't want to be the poor girl. the next time i went to my dads house i asked to sleep on the couch, but my dad made reasons for me not to "you will get cold, we don't have enough blankets, why silly girl, don't you want to sleep next to your nice warm daddy." i was to scared to stand up for myself and could not come up with any excuses. nothing beyond, "i want to sleep by myself. "a few months later, the house burnt down, someone left the heater on. i think it was my grandmother, maybe something in her mind told her the house had bad feelings in it, and one of her voices told her to turn the heat all the way up and walk out the door. i didn't have to go back there very much. i'm glad the house is gone. that i never have to go there again. this was all so many years ago, but i still have the same fear. when i am ever in the room with my father i feel his hot sticky nicotine breath and i feel like i just want to crawl, backing to the wall and leave him laying on the bed wondering why his daughter hates him. i don't want to laugh at his jokes, but it's so hard, as for the most part we have the same sense of humor. i want to hate him, but he has helped make me what i am. with out him touching me i would not have the same level of understanding.

11

i want to hold him at a
distance; i want him to say he is sorry, and not just ever the phone
when he is drunk, like that one time last year. trying to say he was
sorry for the times at the old house; i don't want to feel sorry from
him when he says her was lonely. i don't want to act like i don't know
what he is talking about, i want to say, fuck you dad, you ruined me,
and made all my time growing up tainted with fear. i want to yell and
scream and kick his face push him far far away. i want to pour all my
hate all over him and let it rot at his soul. i don't want to forgive
him. but i almost do. how would it feel to know you raped your child?

O X O X O X O X

imagine it. i had a friend in middle school who's father raped
her..... he shot himself in the head, twice before he was dead. i want
my dad to do that. i don't want him to be alive and sing the blues and
drink every night because of guilt. i don't want him to talk about how
rapists on TV need to die. i want him to stand up to every girl, every
woman, every boy, every man, every gender less/gender queer person,
every fucking human on this earth who has ever been raped, touched or
just felt scared because they have to live in a world where rape is
real and say he is fucking sorry. SORRY.

once i was at value village, and i bought a set of the same sheets of father had, i remembered them from my past. but it wasn't until i laid them on my bed and tried to sleep that i remember where they had come from. i had to rip them off the bed and throw them away before i could sleep. just thinking about it makes my skin feel tight. when my younger sister was visiting my house, when i lived with my father still, she noticed the pillow case my father still has and said. "oh dad, i love those sheets, i still have the other pillow case you gave me. i love you." i couldn't believe that anyone could look at that print and feel anything but terror. baby baby i'm so sorry. there was no way you where going to escape. i promise not to make any jokes any more. what happened was not funny. no, not at all.

mix tapes, tweed skirts, medicine cabinets, tea cakes, mushrooms, snails, nail polish, star stickers, Alice in wonderland, finding old books, strawberry shaped things, glitter, fairies, kelp forests, tea cups, hot baths, kinderwhore, second hand any things

march 30. chapter one.

i was able to not see it, not to deal with it. by making it just a joke. something silly that happened when i was younger. i feel it the shame and the hate and guilt and everything. always. when i am drinking and want to fuck, when i am kissed by someone i don't want to be kissing. when i let my lipstick smear and when i listen to music with voices that are shrill. when i think about Kathleen Hanna and her running for the sheets. when i have to talk to my family. when my father looks at me, at all. but mostly when he looks me in the eye. when our eyes meet i feel like i am going to vomit that he still sees me as a little small thing he can fuck with, one that he can touch and rape over and over again in his mind. like when i was little and he used to tickle me from across the room. that one time when we played the game when he would look in the windows. when he mistook my laughter for glee, instead of the terror that it was. i hate that every man that walks by makes me think of him. i hate that sometimes, while laying in bed, i feel him. i hate that people i truly love make me scared and i can't trust anyone. i hate that when i am fucking i think of him, and anytime anyone tells me anything about there fathers, i want to ask if they where raped.

i hate that i have been in relationships that where abusive. i don't really know what all of this means, i don't think i will ever get over this. i just want to keep writing until my fingers fall of and my heart stops hurting. i hate that i am scared to have children because i don't want to do things, bad things to them. i hate that i am scared that i am going to far when i hug little kids. i hate that i never wanted to hold a baby, ever. because i felt tainted. i hate that every new friend ship is ruined because some where along the line i have to tell them that my father raped me. i hate that i can never trust anyone enough to tell them about my bother. brother. just the word makes me sick. i hate it all so much. i hate the feeling of trying to be asleep so he would just stop kissing me. i hate remembering the feeling of his sick sick lips on my breast. i wish that never ever came to be and that i didn't feel so fucking gross because of it. i hate that i was used sexually because i didn't know how to be friends any other way. i have had sex with most of my friends. very few i have not. that fucking sucks. i hate that i get so sad. i hate that i don't have any security. i think about it all to much. i want to change and help others. i want to talk to him about it, but i fear that he will just laugh and make some joke. *hey dude, remember that one time i totally made out with my sister. " i hate that, incest it funny. and that people joke about it. but i do. i make jokes. sometimes things are just funny, right? it seems so normal that my father did that, but the real problem is this brother. the real point of this all is working through my fear of them when i was older. not the first pain of it, but later, not wanting to shower when anyone was home, that i would not use the same soap that had touched there gross bodies.

that lindy thought my dad was perverted because he said he loved me more than her. that i know if her had the choice it would be me he fucked every night. that by starving myself i would have a body he doesn't like. if i have no breasts he could not compare them to my mothers *rack* fuck you dad. fuck you derrick for taking advantage of my need to please and not having a way to express any sort of emotions other than *fuck me* fuck you both for me not being able to have any real relationships. how is any of this coping? i want to have music, i want to make noise, but i am not confident in anything it do. i always feel like people are making fun of me. i like that i am able to take the emotions out of sex, as it makes me better in bad relationships. but what's the point of being able to take abuse, when one can't take any sort of love with out doubt. how am i supposed to feel good. how am i supposed to be a good person. i should not let myself get wrapped up in pretty things, and moss and little toys, i need to face everything. i need to stand up and start some shit and i need some advice, from someone i love and trust, i love books, but they don't really talk back. i need to just have some support in the form of other people who have been abused. i this is hard, i am drawing a blank and feel like i don't have more to say. i don't know how theses things have shaped me, it's hard to think about it all at once, and it's hard to talk about it. i want to just have it all laid out and i should have done this right after i read this chapter. i would to work through it. i want to write and write and write some more. i want to write a song that will inspire someone to speak.

i have a big voice and i will not spelling.......i should talk about that. i am scared of spelling. i hate it. every time i have to spell, i get feel with so much shame i am to kill myself. i can't spell. i know i am scared of it because my dad would always help me with my spelling when he was drunk and he would make me sleep in his bed. i can't believe he would do something like that. i hate asking what i letters go where, i hate the idea of people reading when i write. i am ashamed of my handwriting. it makes me unable to take notes at meetings, and makes me think that people think i am just lazy. it makes me unable to write notes, and makes me think i sound stupid when i write, because i have to reword everything so i can use only simple words. i hate it. ✗

Mom part one

i don't blame my mother for what my father and my brother did. i
don't blame her for not knowing. i don't blame where for sending me
off on the weekends to my fathers house. i want that to be perfectly
clear. there was no real way she could know. i never told her, never
ever hinted that anything was wrong. at least not at the time. that
said:

my mother is the master of denial. when i was older i made it
painfully clear to her that i was hurting. once when i was in eighth
grade i went to take a shower. i cut my arms and legs with a razor
and peeled all my scabs and let the bleed down my body. i was about
to get under the water and be clean, and my mom walked in. she took a
long look at me. and shut the door. she never asked me why i was
bleeding. i always wondered why she never said anything about it.
once she read a journal i had. not really a dairy. but a little scrap
book. i had pasted a piece of fabric with my blood all over it in to
the book. i saw her reading it. i saw her frown and than nothing but
silence followed. once we went to Hawaii. me her and my sister. i
stop cutting myself for about a month before the trip. the last thing
i wanted was to have hot sand in my wounds and my sister asking about
it. but i had some pretty large/noticeable scars. i wanted to cover
myself, but the heat got the best of me. my mother asked "when did
you start that little nervous tick?" i looked at the sand and she
handed me another beer. that's all that was said. i was 17. she never

18

When you go to bed at night,

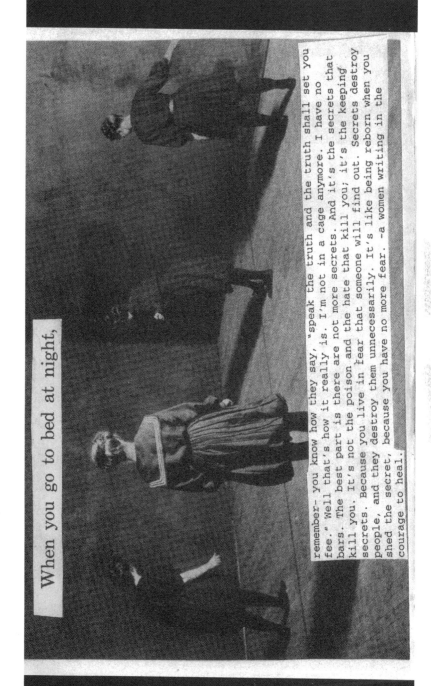

remember- you know how they say, "speak the truth and the truth shall set you free." Well that's how it really is. I'm not in a cage anymore. I have no bars. The best part is there are not more secrets. And it's the secrets that kill you. It's not the poison and the hate that kill you; it's the keeping secrets. Because you live in fear that someone will find out. Secrets destroy people, and they destroy them unnecessarily. It's like being reborn when you shed the secret, because you have no more fear. -a women writing in the courage to heal.

OXOX

i could never trust anyone. still can't. i can't really have a good bath because i feel like someone is watching. i can't sleep with out hiding under the blankets until i fall asleep. i can't tell people about my family. this is always in the way. i have been unable to do/to know what's best for me. i have never been able to hug my family. at least, with out wanting to puke. i hate being touched, or rather i hate being touched by some people, or sometime i just get stiff and want to run. i have felt compation with other people that have been abused. i have wanted to one-up them.

shame shame shame.......

i have lied about it. when i was in middle school, a group of friends where talking about our family members who had abused us. i told them that a man raped me when i was camping. i didn't know who he was. i wonder if any of them remember that. i wonder if any of them don't want to go camping because it's always i the back of there mind. some where, sometime someone i know was raped while camping. i wish i would have just told the truth. it was my father, my brother. i hate that i lied. i lost my ability to know truth. i always wanted some one to come save me. blame it on a love of fairy tales if you like. but i still always hunt out the person with dark hair...some tall dark hansom prince to save me from all of this. i don't need to waste my time like this. i retreat wasting time. i lost anyway of feeling safe. my mother left me with he cares shifted away from the five year old girl crying in her dark room, they shifted over to cocaine, to alcohol. i don't think i want to be around alcohol any more. i lost anyway of asking for help. i always feel like someone is going to forget me in the car. i have nightmares. mostly of rabbits. sometimes i start sweating and my heart beats so fast it's busting out of my chest and i feel like i'm going to die when someone talks about rabbits. i want to take time to think about all of these things. if i could i would stay far far away from all my family. sometimes i think about telling them all.

writing a open letter to my father and my mother and my brother and to the ex-boyfriend that would bully me into sex. that would tell me he wanted to smash his face in because i was so mean and heartless because i didn't want to fuck him that one time. how would read my diary and blame me for writing things that where wrong. that i had some how been a bad person for writing about just about anything. i want to say good time to all the time i spend editing my dairy, my journal so he would no really know how i felt. i want to write a big fuck you letter to my father for causing me to not having better judgments. why would you ever teach your child that the one who loves her also will hurt her. why would you teach the lesson that yelling and raping and rejection are ok, as long as you love the person. i want to tell him that because of him i have laid back many time and let people fuck because it's so much easier than saying no. i wish my family was dead. all of them. well, maybe not the "good" sister. the one that cut her wrist and had to get stitches when she was in high school. mom would just make jokes about it. fuck your stupid jokes mom. she does not have "nervous tick, and nether do i. we are cutting ourselves because there is no fucking way out. i wish i never had to think of them ever again. i wish i was able to shut them out for good. when i was in middle school i always said regret is a wasted emotion, and that once one starts to regret things they have done, they are dead. i think i truly wanted to believe that the best people never made real mistakes, and that if they did they would learn from the mistake, and move on. i'm not sure if i still believe that. but i want to learn from these mistakes and move on. but i don't see anything beyond this. i regret letting him fuck me in the woods behind the church, and i never asked him why. i don't want to ever ever let someone do that to me again. i just don't know how to not let it happen again.

my father married a woman. i remember the first time i met my future
stepbrothers. we went to my soon to be step mother house. it was
snowing out. me and derrick (the middle son, about my age) played
dirty word Scrabble and had a pen war. it was fun. more than fun it
was great. my father and stepmother courted for a year or so before
the got married. some point, so after the marriage, i moved in with
them.i was in sixth grade. i shared a room with the younger of the
sons, and everything was fine. my mother was under the impression
that my father would be a better parent. i suppose she was right, at
the time all my mother seemed to have time fro was her boyfriend,
drinking, and what ever drug was hot at the moment. derrick was
always making fun of me, my music, my hair, my tits, my boyfriend,
anything was far game. he would sneak into my room and steal things
from me, my journal, my money, my tapes, my underwear, anything he
wanted. he would try to get me in trouble as much as he could, making
up lies about me. planting things in my room for my step mother to
find later. we where in the same class at school, and he would tease
me and basically make my life hell. i was so scared of my
step-mother, she was always yelling at me and being unpretickable.
sometimes sweet as pie, the next moment screaming because i looked
like a whore. my father was no help, if i asked him for anything, he
would just ask me to sit on his lap. or put his stinking heavy arm
around me as i tried to pretend that i couldn't smell the mind
blurring patchouly oil he always wore. as much as i could i hid in
my room listing to the radio, or playing my nirvana tape, over and
over. spring turned to summer, as it tends to do. we got a new house
one much grander than the last. over one hundred years old,

"Oh, thank you," said Cinderella.

simi-rotting but amazing. i had my own room, but it was still open
season on me. then, one day, derrick starting being nice. he would
tell jokes and for once, they where not about me. we would talk about
songs we both liked, maybe i wasn't so bad after all. i just wanted
him to be nice to me. i wanted him to stop stealing and just be my
friend. one night, i was in his room talking, and he pulled back the
blanket, to show me his hard-on. i left. somehow i tricked myself
into believing that it was a mistake and that he didn't mean to.
later that summer, we went camping, and being kids, my two new
brothers and i slept in a tent faraway from out parents. i still
don't have a memory of how it started, but at some point, derrick is
rubbing me between the legs and kissing my neck. i was so scared. i
wish i knew how it happened. i wish i knew how to make it stop. i do
remember thinking, i hope he is nice to me now. he stopped, after a
while. the next morning, he acted as if nothing had happened, if
anything he was meaner than ever before. at one point, we were both
on the deck of the cabin and i asked him how he was doing. he told me
to fuck off. to not talk to him, or people would know what happened.
i only wanted to be his friend, or t least his sister. he drove off
on his bike and was gone a few hours. that night, i slept in the van
with my younger brother, Charles. derrick said he was going to sleep
in the woods again. sometime in the night derrick came in the van
and started touching me as i lay there trying to be asleep. he was
rubbing my ceast and trying to pull my shirt up. i sat up and let him
kiss me. *dear god, i want him to be nice to me. * then i laid down
and let him pull my shirt up. i let him suck my tits and rub his
fucking dick on my leg. then i closed my eyes and pretended to be
asleep. after while he stopped and never tried anteing again. i lived
with them for years, never telling anyone. he always stole from me,
money, tapes, cds, anything he wanted. i was to scared to tell him

not to. once he smashed a piece of my art work i had worked hours on. stomped on it. smashed the glass and left it in the center of my newly cleaned room. we where home alone. he would lie and tear my posters off the wall and into bits. he would rip pages out of my dairy. so i stopped writing. all through high school i never had a journal. never had anyone i felt i could talk to, at least not fully. there where always lies holding me back. things i couldn't bring up. this is one of them.

They ripped off the sash

and pulled off the beads.

Yes, summer days

are long, long days.

mom part two

was someone i could trust with anything, let alone secrets and shame. i hate hugging her. i remember once, when i was young, (over seven, younger than ten) i was sick and she asked if i wanted to sleep in he room. i yelled and asked her why i would ever want t do that. wasn't that something bad kids did? but i yelled at her allot. i yelled at her for coming home late, or not at all. i yelled at her when she didn't wake me up. when i was in grade school i told every one that my mom was a whore. to my young mind it seemed like she was. not coming home at nights or all sorts of strange men sleeping over. once i stole some of her drugs to show the kids at recess. she caught me with it before i left the house. i was not aloud to go to school that day. i had to sit at home alone. i never once told her i ever got pregnant. when i was 16 and had a miscarriage. i listened to her cry about my older sisters abortion. i listened to her cry in the car about the grandchild that she would never had. i was bleeding all over my skirt and i never told her. i wonder how she would feel if she knew i have been pregnant five times. or if she would make a joke about me being a slut. i feel as though i have always hated her. she always disappointed me. on just about every level a person can. she never sexually abused me. but she never showed that she cared. only i super guilt trip ways has she ever given me anything. maybe that's not fully true. i every thing is tainted with some sticky badness. even that trip to Hawaii was a fucking sham. i have never wanted to go there. never expressed any interest in that part of the county at all. i don't like the heat, i don't like the sun, i don't like touests, fancy hotels, rental cars, views of sunsets, overpriced cocktails or seafood. i don't remember one thing i ate there.

i wish i could take you out and buy you treats and sing with you, and play in the park and take time to do all the fun things you never did. i wish that i could take back time and play out side with you, instead of hiding in that big chair watching reruns of the Adams family. i wish you could have changed you name to W and gotten the black dress with the white collar. i would like to tell you that you didn't have to be tough all the time, and it's ok to want friends. it's ok to want someone to hold you. i would tell you that it's ok to dance, and even if it hurts, it's worth it. i would tell you to try to stand up for yourself more. and that it's ok to be rejected sometimes. it doesn't mean you are worthless. i would like to take back all the times i told you where no good and that everyone hates a fat ugly girl like you. i would like to show you that you where not stupid. i would like to talk to you, remember that one time when you pulled jenny's hair and puked on he little shoes in the lunch line. was that a few weeks after you tried to tell you're friend that your father molested you? is that why you puked at the sight of Seth with his big arms around little jenny? is that why you where not friend with her anymore? i want to tell you father to go fucking die. i would tell your mom about what was going on. or that time when you where 12 and mom didn't want to talk to us because she was to busy taking drugs with her stupid boyfriend who chased us around the house with the big knife.

about how she slapped you in the face for calling her selfish? my back huts and i don't know why i'm writing this now. last night, i was reading the chapter, and the idea of writing a letter to yourself as a child seemed so stupid. but i can't stop crying. every thing just pushes the tears out of my eyes. maybe it's a good thing. i can't tell yet. i don't want people to ask me what my zine is about when tell them i am working on one. i don't want the silence to fill the space. greedy silence. i want you to have a house where it's ok to wear anything. and not have some creepy dad checking you out. when i was in middle school my dad would ask me to pick things of for him. i could feel him watching and even as i wanted to pull his hair and puke on his fucking face, i couldn't stand the thought of being any closer to him. i wonder if he, ever wondered why i always sat to far to the edge of my seat in the car. i would take you far away. i am sorry i have not been good. i'm sorry i play it off. it didn't hurt when mom said she couldn't afford you. but somehow always has a new car. a new weeding ring. i'm sorry i make jokes about the lonely time you spent praying to a god you never believed in. "please mom.. come home tonight." i would want to know what was really going on when you didn't come home those afternoons and the police where called. what you felt when you mother slapped you in the face and called you a brat from lying to her. "but mom, i tried to call you." i would tell you friend sally to stop teaching you and stop asking about sex. i always wondered how she knew so much about sex. i think i would have asked her, if i·had not been so afraid. i hate that i never cared of you. that i never did any of the projects you wanted to. i never painted, never let you learn how to shape things with clay, never let you use crayons i was always to scared to let any evidence of myself. i would teach you how to spell and how to do math. i would let you cry when ever you needed to, used of hiding and yelling all the time. i spend so much of my younger years just watching tv. i was so hard to have friends and have to do anything. so hard to run, to ride bikes, to doing anything that meant someone might have the chance to look at my body. it was so much better to eat top rammen and watch tv from 12 noon to bedtime.

27

don't point out mistakes.

don't pretend like you never read this.

talk to me about it.

tell me a secret

don't ever make jokes about it

give me a hug

don't tell me how much you hate my dad.

It

doesn't help.

this is my favorite picture of myself.

once someone asked me who it was. they said it didn't look a thing like me.

that i looked like a boy.

my father hates boys.

baby

fever.

i want to have kids. more to the point i want to have one. Soon. Now. the idea of it is completely absurd at this point in my life. i am in school. i have no job. no money. well, very little money that is given to me by my father every month to pay my rent. i will be rich soon. if rich means getting $175 from my tax return. i feel ashamed for wanting to have a baby. selfish and like someone will think i am trapped for wanting this. i can't even talk to the person i love about it. i have to write about it in this. rewrote this section a few times over. what if i was an abuser? what if i was compelled to molest my baby, my child? what if i hit them or was simply cold with them as they grew up? what if having a child made me hate myself more than ever. how would anything ever work out. i feel like even bringing it up or talking it with my voice with cause worlds to rip apart and every one will leave me. once there was great talk of having babies. getting pregnant and giving birth. but that ended in my second abortion. ended in my looking at the fetus with it's rib cage ripped in two. i know it's not the right thing to want. at least not right for my life, for my relationship, for anything now. but i feel my life speeding to the end with no way real way to slow it down. maybe having a child would give me the strength to stand up to my father to my whole family and tell them no more. "this friendship is over mom." or "dad, you are a rapist, and you will not ever bee near my child." people are much better at protecting their babies than themselves. right? maybe not. but that's what all the parenting books and Martha Stewart baby issues seem to say.

mom part three

she
bought me a plane ticket with even caring weather or not i wanted to
go. i few months earlier she asked me if i could go anywhere where
would it be. new york. of course. most of my family lives there. i
always want to go there. but instead, i was selfish and spoiled and a
bad kid if i didn't go to Hawaii. i ended up sunburnt and crossing
my arms hated her more than ever. hating her as she got wasted at the
beach and flirted with my sisters boyfriend. i few years later, when
i live was not much more than lists of numbers, she reacted in a way
that made me sick. i was starving myself. i would cut myself if i had
been "good" and not eaten more than 200 calories a day. reowrd. i
would cut myself if i went over and was "bad". punishment. it didn't
mater. i still got what i really wanted. my life was over if i eat
to much. tears and punches all over my body. bad. fat. whore. but i
lost weight. i didn't see my mother much. that day, at her house i
ate in one meal more than i had in the past two weeks. i was on the
edge of puking it all back up, and she can into the bathroom and
asked me what my secret was. i asked dumbly, "what do you mean?" you
are so thin. i am jealous, i am fat, and i want to look like you. i
told her to stop eating cheese. what a fucking cop out.

"No," said Cinderella sadly. "I did not

have any time to fix MY dress."

32

thank you to (almost) everyone who
ever lived at villa kulla or the flamingo flat.

thank you to Ellen Bass and Laura Davis.

thank you to heavens to betsy and bikini kill.

thank you to Caroline Marigold, April Cordelia

thank you
oxoxoxoxoxoxo

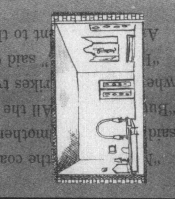

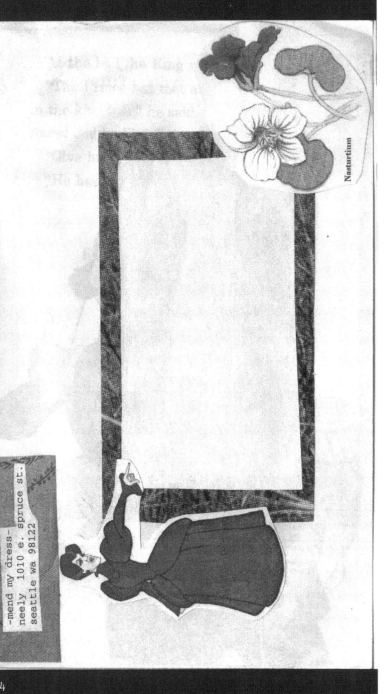

-mend my dress-
neely 1010 e. spruce st.
seattle wa 98122

Nasturtium

DEAR STEPDAD:
the letters never sent.

by: neely bat chestnut.

dear stepdad:

you where a total jerk.

fuck you and your shitty family.

i am glad you went to jail.

i am also glad you are dead.

fuck you.

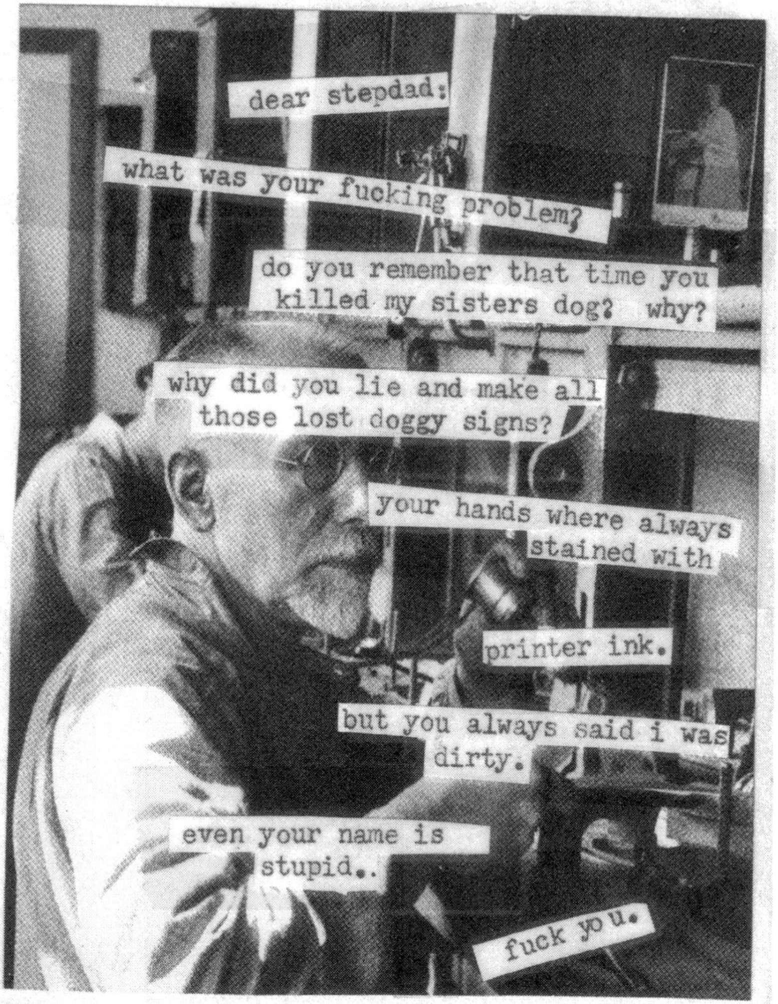
dear stepdad:
what was your fucking problem?
do you remember that time you killed my sisters dog? why?
why did you lie and make all those lost doggy signs?
your hands where always stained with
printer ink.
but you always said i was dirty.
even your name is stupid..
fuck you.

dear stepdad:

it was fun x when you dyed my
hair that one time, boy, was mom
pissed off. it was also fun when
made jokes with that funny voice,
but other times i didnt like yo u
so much. like that time you where
high and cased me around the house
in yourunderwear

i was scared of
knives for along time after that.
i also thought it was weird that you
thought Courtney Love was hot.
i really didnt like you at all when
you and my mom would shootherion
together. me and my sister totally
knew. i felt sorry for you when me
and my mom would buy you wine so
you could get up in the morning.

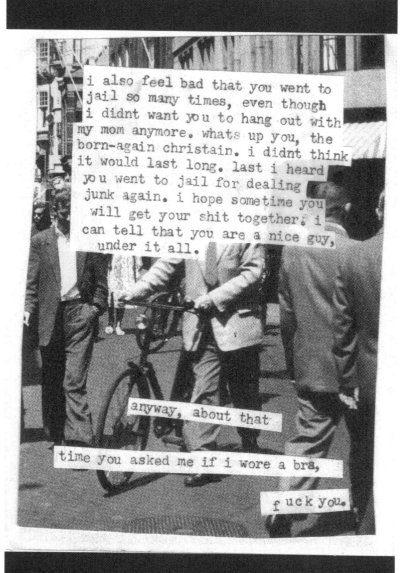

i also feel bad that you went to
jail so many times, even though
i didnt want you to hang out with
my mom anymore. whats up you, the
born-again christain. i didnt think
it would last long. last i heard
you went to jail for dealing
junk again. i hope sometime you
will get your shit together. i
can tell that you are a nice guy,
under it all.

anyway, about that

time you asked me if i wore a bra,

f uck you.

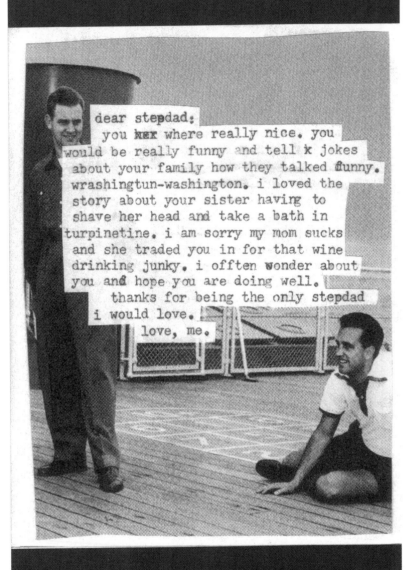

dear stepdad:
  you wer where really nice. you
would be really funny and tell k jokes
about your family how they talked funny.
wrashingtun-washington. i loved the
story about your sister having to
shave her head and take a bath in
turpinetine. i am sorry my mom sucks
and she traded you in for that wine
drinking junky. i offten wonder about
you and hope you are doing well.
  thanks for being the only stepdad
i would love.
     love, me.

dear stepdad:

by the time you came i the
sceen i was to old to really
bother with you to much.
but, wow, you are a fuck up.
you treat your kids like shit,
you hardly even look twice when
your five year old was crying,
and scratching her eyes out.

you where mostlikely high on
crack at the time, but damn.
yu treaded my mom like shit too,
even after she more or less raised
your kid and cooked you three meals
a day for over fiveyears. i cant
believe she stayed with you for so
long. if you only knew all the mean
things we said about you. wow.
fuck you.

dear stepdad:
you are the newest in
a long line of fuck ups
my mom has decided to take into
her life and home. you dont
seem to bad. good luck.
i bet you will not last five
years.

the end.

i   also do a zine called mend
my dress.

#one is writings
about
#two is short writings   incest.
about diffrent
homes i have lived in

both can be ordered
for $I and a
6653 CARLETON AVE S   60 cent stamp
SEATTLE, WA 98108.

neely_ohara at hellokitty.com

42

Querido padrastro
las cartas nunca enviadas

Zine por Neely Bat Chesnut
(originalmente en ingles)

Querido padrastro:

eras un idiota completo.
~~jerk.~~

~~fuck~~ Que se jodan
tu y tu familia de mierda.

i am que hayas ido a la cárcel.

También me ~~glad you are~~
alegra que estés muerto.

fu Jódete.

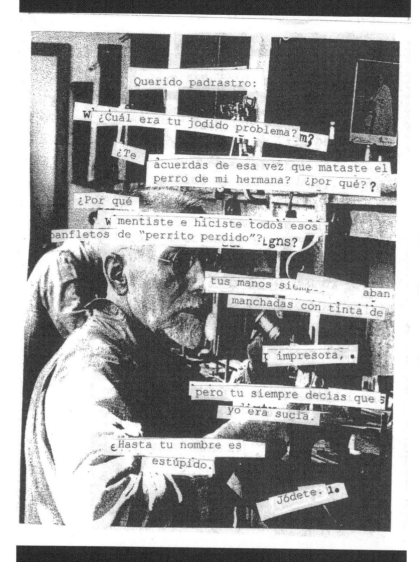

Querido padrastro:

¿Cuál era tu jodido problema?

¿Te acuerdas de esa vez que mataste el perro de mi hermana? ¿por qué?

¿Por qué mentiste e hiciste todos esos panfletos de "perrito perdido"?

tus manos siempre estaban manchadas con tinta de impresora,

pero tu siempre decías que yo era sucia.

Hasta tu nombre es estúpido.

Jódete.

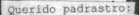

Querido padrastro:

it was fun x when you dyed my

Fue divertido cuando me teñiste el
cabello esa vez, vaya, mamá se enojó de
verdad. También era divertido cuando
hacías bromas con esa voz divertida,
pero otras veces, no me gustabas mucho.
Como esa vez que estabas drogado y me
perseguiste por la casa en tu ropa
interior. ased me around the house
in your underwear

i was scared of

knife. Le tuve miedo a los cuchillos
por mucho tiempo después de eso.
También pensaba que era raro que tu
pensaras que Courtney Love estaba
buena. De verdad no me gustaba para
nada cuando tu y mi mamá se inyectaban
heroína. Mi hermana y yo lo sabíamos.
También me sentía mal cuando ibas a
prisión, a pesar de que ya no te quería
cerca de mi mamá.
you could get up in the morning.

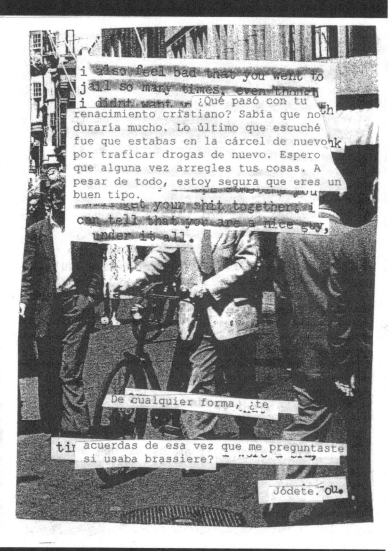

i also feel bad that you went to
jail so many times, even though
i didnt want ... ¿Qué pasó con tu
renacimiento cristiano? Sabía que no
duraría mucho. Lo último que escuché
fue que estabas en la cárcel de nuevo
por traficar drogas de nuevo. Espero
que alguna vez arregles tus cosas. A
pesar de todo, estoy segura que eres un
buen tipo.
... get your shit together. i
can tell that you are a nice guy,
under it all.

De cualquier forma, ¿te
acuerdas de esa vez que me preguntaste
si usaba brassiere?

Jódete. ou.

dear stepdad:

Querido padrastro:
Eras muy simpatico. Solías ser muy
divertido y contra historias sobre tu
familia y como ellos hablaban raro. Me
encantaba la historia en la cual tu
hermana se tuvo que afeitar la cabeza y
bañarse en trementina. Siento mucho que
mi mamá apeste y que te haya cambiado
por el drogadicto que bebía vino. A
veces me pregunto por ti y espero que
te esté yendo bien. Gracias por ser el
único padrastro que amaría. Con amor.
Yo.

i would love.
love, me.

Querido padrastro: by the time you came i the

Para el momento en el cual llegaste a la escena, yo era ya muy mayor para preocuparme mucho. Pero, wow, sí que estabas jodido! Tratabas a tus niños como mierda. Casí ni miraste cuando tu niño de cinco años estaba llorando y casi sacándose los ojos. Seguramente estabas drogado en crack en ese

you where mostlikely high on

momento, pero, maldición, trataste también como mierda a mi mamá, incluso después que ella crió a tus niños y te cocinó tres comidas al día por cinco años. No puede creer que ella se haya quedado contigo por tanto tiempo. Si solo supieras todas las cosas malas que decíamos de ti. Wow. Jódete.

things we said about you. wow. fuck you.

dear stepdad:

Querido padrastro: e newest in
Tu eres el más nuevo en la larga lista
de cagadas que mi mamá ha decidido
dejar entrar a casa y en su vida. no
pareces ser tan malo. Buena suerte. Te
apuesto a que no duras cinco años. El
fin. i bet you will not last five
years.

the end

i   also do a zine called mend
        my dress.

                #one is writings
                        about
two is short writings   incest.
about diffrent
homes i have lived in

                both can be ordered
                for $I and a
                60 cent stamp

6653 CARLETON AVE S
SEATTLE, WA 98108.

neely_ohara at hellokitty.com

MEND MY DRESS

by neely bat chestnut.

#2

i can not even bring myself to visit the side of town where we used to live.

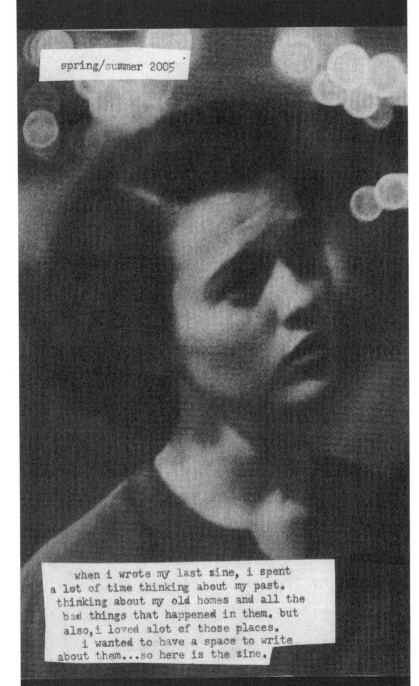

spring/summer 2005

when i wrote my last zine, i spent
a lot of time thinking about my past.
thinking about my old homes and all the
bad things that happened in them. but
also, i loved a lot of those places.
i wanted to have a space to write
about them...so here is the zine.

        my first memory takes place
here, my father and mother fighting.
 my father walking outside, to smoke.
 i was held in his arms, and i can xx
 recall him saying that he would leave,
 but not with out me. later, when i was
 around four i would sit in a xkxx chair
or walk around and around the small
      living room. mostly alone, i felt like
      i owned that house. i would day dream
 hoping that my mother would die, and the
 house would be left to me.i was born there,
 and it x only seemed fair that i could
 die there two.i think living in the
  house where i was born made death seem
 all the more closer. my grandmother died
 in my childhood bedroom. but that was long
 before i was ever born. when i was in grade
 school i thought of all sorts of ways she
 had met her death. all i was told was that
 she had died too young. i pictured my
   grand father, crazy with saddness
   burning her clothes and sending the
     ashes to sea in a sail boat. xxxxxxx .
     the old house was built by his family,
 sometime in the very last bit of the
 x 19th century. marble counter tops.
  no heat, save the tiny stove in the
 living room.the house has vines and
    blackberries under the front door.
   the bottom half was totaly rottedwxxx
 away, so we just used the back door.
    there was a ball room, with huge oil
 paintings of theold dead family, and
 a grand paino with termites and beetles
 living in it. feeding on the rotting
 ivory. a stuffed crab in the entryway.
    stained glass of dragons.

sometimes sand would come out of the
drains, sometimes frogs. it was always cold.
once, i feet fell in to the stove. burning
my arm. cooking it, leaving a sheet of skin
behind. my grandfather sold the house,
and we had to move. i was in second grade
and i didnt understand. i hated the rich
family from CA that where buying the place,
only to tear it down. i watched my beloved
home turn to a pile of scrap. watched the xx
rooms be burned. i miss the house. when i
younger, i always wanted to build the house
just like it. follow the plans, making
everytihng just so, but with myself
aging, i understand that the things that
made the house so wonderful can not be
faked. age and neglect only work that
sort of xxjix.magic.

i like to
imagine my
grandmother
looking like
this before
her death
at age 36.
missing someone
you never met
where able
meet sure is a
strange feeling.

before i was two,
my father was kicked
out of the house,
thus:

OTHER STRANGE PLACES
MY FATHER CALLED
HOME.

for awhile my dad lived in
the basement of a party house, in
a small town, i dont remeber much,
the teenage girl upstairs
listening to Bananarama alot,
my grandmother sleeping down the hall,
Laying on the floor and being read horror
comics before sleep. i think he only
lived there a few months.

*   *   *   *   *

the next house was across the
street, it was dark and scary. so
cold we would have to heat our drinks
in the winter, if they where left out
they would be frozen solid. i think
the walls where wood siding. i can recall
my sister watching 21 jump street and
teasing her hair, cut jeans and an ugly
scuzzy boyfriend. most of what i remebe r
of that house was writne in my first
issue. my grandmother caused the house
to burn down. it was the end of second
grade when the house died.

*   *   *   *   *

for about five years my fatherlived with
a woman, mad she was. ten years older than
him with a grandchild my age, her house
was a dream house.

she had a horse and trees with flowers
all year round.
french doors, books in piles all over,
a large yard, a pretty skylight over her
bed. i slept in a hammock near her bed.
i still lived with my mom, and her
house was a nice excape. i loved washing her
windows with newspaper.

we moved in right after the house
sold, it was /is one of those factory
m ade jobs with ¤¤ boring walls, and
cheap everything. i had grown up with
marble and hard wood floors, i was not
happy about the new house at all. but a
at age eight, i could not fully
express why.the land it was put on
was muddy and boring. my most ¤¤¤¤¤
vivid memory of the house where the
long afternoons when i was
alone.

sitting watching after school
cartoons. sometimes i would eat piles
of food, mostly with my bare hands
hiding under the bar. eatting untill
i was sick and then i would pry more
out, and some how force even more into
my mouth. sometimes i would try to
vomit, but mostly i just felt guilty.
at the dinnertable, my mother and
sister would always pick food off my
plate. mocking my slow pace. its a
long running joke that carries over to
this day. sometimes on the phone, my mom
will make some side comment. "oh, your
eatting right now, ill call back next
week. " ha-fucking-ha mom. i wanted so
much to be more like my sister. once she
moved out, i got her room. i had the same
same ¤ walls, b ut i was still not as
cool as her.we had those shitty fake lace
curtins and neon lighting. i hate that hot
house, and was glad to move out when i
did. even if it ment living with my

father and crazy step-mother.
my mother is always wanting me to move
back "home" yeah, as if that shithole
was even "mine". i would have nightmares
or more "daymares" that some one would co
come in and kidnap me while i was Alone
my mother was so excited to live in a
clean new home, but when i was a child
i didnt understand why anyone would ever
trade xxix oak and ceder of partical
board.

now that i am a little older, i can understad
understand her a little more. i can see
the positive side of having a house that
is not totally falling apart. the small
joy in always have plain water come from
the taps. the walls are all one color, and
there are no spirts hxxx wandering about,
keeping you up at night. i can see that it
would feel nice to live in a house void of
death and memories. we could never wear
shoes in the h ouse. we could not do alot
of fun thi ngs. in that house i learned
to hate xxxxix carpet.

i had a little
roomand a side closet room. it was about
half the size of my room at the old house,
and i didnt like it.i didnt ever like the
house. but i lived there for a little over
four years. my mom still lives there, and
and exhusband built an apartment next to it.
im sure that some time i will live there
agai n. but that place always feels like a
trap.

THE KVI COTTAGE:

the little summer beach house style   house was
supper cute. it was light blue, witha breakfast nook, a big
yard with huge trees. we tied a rope swing and it made for
summer long fun. my father lived there withhis new wife and
her two xx sons.over the summer after fifth grade i lived
there for a few months. my new step mother gave me pretty
flowered curtins and i slept on the floor. my room was under the
stairs, and had a niceview of the little roads. from the
upstairs window you could see the KVI radio towers,and it
was a short walk to the KVI beach . the beach had fireworks.

there was a large fig tree in
a empty lot near by. big leaves
ripe fruit all the time, or so it
seemed. xxxxxxty a pack of kids
hanging out all the time. heading
home only to drink koolaid and
eat grilled cheese.

i felt so much older than
every one,i was the only one who
cared about music.

there where crabs and little fish at the beach. sunburns
and gxt girls in bikinis. i loved that little house.
it was the small time when everything seemed nice with thaxt
famliy. before my stepmother started being the classic
evil stepmother. before my stepbrothers xxxxxx disliked my
father. but they didnt live there long, and the honeymoon was
soon over. some family moved in. there kids where much cleaner
than us. the wife pretty, anf the husband was young. not a
grey hair in sight. and none of the biting sarcasim.

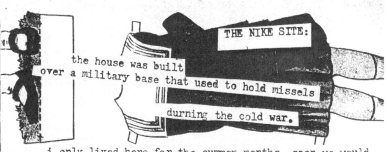

THE NIKE SITE:

the house was built over a military base that used to hold missels durning the cold war.

i only lived here for the summer months, soon we would move to another, much better house.

it was old, but not old enough to be cool or interesting. built in the 50s for military families. windows that would xxx draw moisture to them. it would collect in the window sills and black mold was always growing on them. i moved in to this house at the end of sixth grade. my mother giving up on me. she had put in her time, it was my fathers turn. somehow with his guidance i "would turn out right". my mother never could punish me. i shared a little room with the younger of the two new brothers. early mornings we would get up and watch cartoons before catching the bus. sometimes in the living room we would play RISK. morethan once the game ended in tears it was the smallest house i had ever lived it in. with paper-thin walls. my stepmother loved playing harp badly. and the older brother was always listening to the top 40 radio station. the house had ugly curtains and it smelled like mold and something far morexxxplxxxt unplesant. a young girl who lived down the block would always comeover and want to hang out more offten than not she had a black eye or arms covered in black and blue marks. i always wanted to report her father wherx he would always beat the dog in front of the kids who lived on the block.

but i never did.

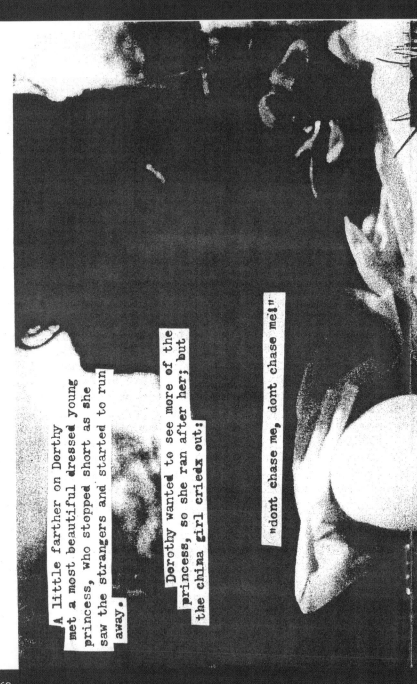

A little farther on Dorthy met a most beautiful dressed young princess, who stopped short as she saw the strangers and started to run away.

Dorothy wanted to see more of the princess, so she ran after her; but the china girl criedx out:

"dont chase me, dont chase mė¦"

She had such a frightened voice that Dorothy stopped and said "Why not?"

"Because," answered the princess, also stopping, a safe distance away, "if i run i may fall down and break myself."

"But couldnt you be mended?"

"Oh, yes; but one is never so pretty after being mended you know," replied the princess.

"I suppose not," said Dorothy.

-L. Frank Baum, The Wizard of Oz.

THE JESUS BARN HOUSE:

picture it. a farmhouse built in 1891
built by a man who owned a saw mill.

the best wood. the richest man. a huge
plot of land with a stream, a lake, forest
feild and everything else one could want, if
it was the turn of the century. a old barn.
picture its the 1960s and you are a jesus
crazy love cult cult. you move in. the house
has been empty for many xxx years. you paint
the word JESUS in bright pink across the barn.
you arange the large rocks in the feild to spell
out JESUS. you want to wake up every morning
and see that word from you bedroom window.

years go by and LSD takes its toll on you r faith
you leave. for years the house is left
alone. some people movein. they are families
with junky mothers and fathers. sometimes whole
families rent out bedrooms. people sell
sex in the house, sometime or another every
one leaves. some people have dogs. the dogs
are left. locked in the house, the kitchen floods
and the back half rotts away. the deck is missing
there is a door on t e second floor that goes
nowhere. a secret room that is borded up.
the house is almost dead. sometime along the
line the sewage line is broken and its been
flowing under the house for years. this is the
house me and my family moved into when i was
12.there where little pink crosses all over.
the barn was gone, it fell in the early 1980s.
we moved in in the summer of 94. i got a large
bedroom upstairs with two walls full of
windows. the small closet had once been a
bedroom for two of the children of the junkies.

i never met them, but if the kids next door
are to believed, the older boy liked to shoot
dogs and shoplift.it was in that house that
"grew up" countless fights with my stepmom.
she and her sons moved in and out II times in
the eight years me and my father lived there.
the househadmany guests scary sounds. voiced
from k nowhere, cats would fluff up and
look at the lost spirts for far to long.
it was a fun place to live in. the first
few years was mosly spent fixing it up, making
it somewhat "nicer". we painted it. the
inside was painted a grotesque hot pink,
the color of candy and rubber brains. we
painted the outside, torn apart the kitchem
and built new floors. more than once or
twice strange old hippies would come by
and want to look around. under a broken step
we found a huge bag of heroin . the fire place
was full of old needles and tubing. it seemed
everyone on the small island hadonce lived the
there, or atleast knew some old stories about it
i thought my father would end up buying the
place, and i could bide my time, wait for
him to die, and move in. living out my
days in a rotting crazy house.

getting to know all the old
spirts, before becoming one myself.

i often though of taking my own life
while i stayed there. sometimes i wish
that i had. but only sometimes.
as i grew up, i had to move out. i was
I9 before i left, it would seem that
i would have gotten out sooner, because
of my father, and everything else. but
i loved that house more that i have
hated anything. in the end, the
owner sold it to a rich man from
L.A. and he lives there now.
sometimes i think of
killing him.

taking what is mine.

When i was 19 i moved from my
fathers house. so here we have:

WEIRD PLACES AND BAD IDEAS:

MEGANS APARTMENT:

me and some friends had been trying to find a house to
live in on Vashon island, (where i had been living)
but we did not have much luck, no one wanted to
rent there nice summer homes to xxx a bunch of
crazy looking kids. i had a friend who was going to
need some one to look after her apartment for a while
when she went to New York for school. me and my pal
took it on and moved in. i was working at a little
bookshop on vashon, so i had to take the ferry
and busses for three hours each way everyday. the place
was tiny, and soon it was shared with yet another
person. three sad people in a one bedroom apartment,
not a great idea. most of the time i was drunk and
wanting to die. i was poor, or i should say; i had
just enough money to pay rent and the bills. my
ferry money, my food, and my beer money was all stolen.

i invited strangers over, and
was more or less a jerk to everyone. my heart
broken, and kept getting more and more broken. i wished
i was dead. when someone wants to die, they dont make
a very good roomate. onc all i can say was the house
was to small, and the time was not right.

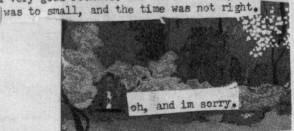

oh, and im sorry.

THE CRAP HOUSE AKA THE DEAD END HOUSE.

after moving out of the little apartment, i went
back to my fathers for the summer. at the end of
summer, me my boyfriend and our friend where looking
for a new place to live. a old friend from middle
school was looking for housemates. it worked great,
and we moved in. the house and time spent there was
the worst ~~ever~~ ever. one of the roomates turned out
to be really into white pride and would boast of
his familys former slave holdings. brag about his
grandfather and fathers involment with the KKK.

looking back, i dont really understand why i
lived there so long. my boyfriend at the time was not
..um..very nice, and i felt trapped. the house had mold
everywhere. books would mold sitting on there shelves.
we lived around the block from a little market, and
the air stank of rotting grease and other such things.
we where robbed a few times. most of my time was spent
hidding in my room, crying or painting my face.

sometimes it didnt seem to bad. when it was just me
and one of the two roomates i did like. through that
house i made one new friend i still keep today.
this house was also one of those rancid 1950s army jobs.
rotting in the most unpleasant way. the house was a
pile of garbage. it had neon lighting and it was just
fuckinggross. i would rather have no home than ever
live in a place like that ever again.

THE VILLA KULA:

i have been trying for a week to find the right
words to express my love for this house.
        i dont think i will ever be able to do it.
a long list of amazing things happed here there.
friends where made and friends lost.

        these pictures will help tell
                a little bit of the story.

this a picture from a party
we had a few years ago.

just two years of living in a house that was
falling apart under us. just two years of roomates
coming and going. it changed and it changed me.
writers block.

the walls where screams in silence

vil

the front of the house.

vincent is pouring water into his lap,

i am making a silly face. the night ended in a couch
through a window and mushrooms
between everyones toes

THE B & B

things change, and no matter hard you hold on,
the past slipps away. i would like to live
some of these house i wrote about,
but i know i cant.but i understand change
is good. i live in a new place now.

i share the house with old and new friends
it looks like we are going to have I2 living here
this summer.

unlike some houses i have lived in, this
one only has good feelings in it. no sad spirts.
its almost summer,and the sun shine feels good.
for once i feel hopeful for x what lies ahead.

the first issue of mend my dress
is still around, and can be ordered
from me for 1$ and a 60 cent stamp.

www.eyecandyzine.com/sweetcandydistro.com
or,
http://northstar.dime-a-dozen.net

thank you to ever one who was so
nice and suportive after
reading my last zine.

thank you ariana for sending
the WIZARD OF OZ

an extra thank you to dashel and ALexis
for the typewriters...xox

LIME ZINE
two stamps—
Arina,
    6066 Shingle Creek
    Pkwy #148
Brooklyn Center
MN 55430

TURPENTINE ZINE
$1 + 60¢ stamp US, $4 outside US, or trade
Turpentine@comcast.net
www.angelfire.com/zine2/turpentine
1182 Juliet Ave. St. Paul MN 55105

neely
6653 carleton ave s
seattle wa 98108

MEND MY DRESS

3

THE LITTLE MATCH GIRL

or,

my dead

grandmother.

by neely bat chestnut.

Early summer 2006

this is all about my grandmother,

she died a few springs ago.

unexpectedly, i

miss her BONITA

SNAP FASTENERS

RUST PROOF   SIZE OO

thank you for reading.

Growing up, i always hated my grandmother. i wanted a fairy godmother that would come and save me, swirl her wand around a bit and melt all my problems away. i hated my grandmother because she wouldn't do that, couldn't do that. i hated her because she was crazy. because she would have visions and she would hear

voices telling her terrible things. i wanted her to see that bad things that where happening to me, not just inside her mind. she seemed so selfish. i was scared of her. she would tell stories of Nazis. she would talk for a long time. telling me lists, numbers of people they had killed. talk of gas chambers and trains full of starving dying people. i

hated her for being born in new york and never having to face those things. she didn't talk much about the other things in her mind. when i was little i hated my grandmother for being scottish and irish. i hated her for being catholic. hated her for talking about god. i hated her for not being a jew. i hated the little beads she was always praying on. i was always scared of the pictures of jesus all over the walls and i hated watching her smoke and drink so

much. she was always smoking. i have a cookie jar she made, and it still had sticky lung paste all over it. it's brown

and covered with lint. it smells like an ashtray. when someone smokes a lot the walls stain with tobacco, but so do the

dishes, the jesus and mary statues the rosaries and the yarn. she would always make all sorts of blankets, and i aways thought they where so ugly. i wanted quilts instead. when she died i stole the quilt off her bed. when she was dying i took the rings off her fingers and i put them on. my father told me too. when i

was younger i always wanted her opal ring, now i have it on my right hand. i feel like i missed out on her life, but she did too. what sort of life did she have?

she was always so sad, scared, unhappy. my grandfather left her and my father after she had her first breakdown. the first time she was sent

to the state medical facility. state run hospital, new york, 1954. i can only begin to think about how scary that place must have been. electroshock therapy, ice water baths, starvation.when she was released, her husband had left her, fleeing to New Orleans. her five year old son had been shipped off to live with her sister and

she had no home. she lived in Greenwich village and made friends with poets and did all sorts of fun things, i'm sure. she never talked about it much. i could never be sure what she was saying was true. i am filled with

guilt. i should have felt love for her and i should have shown it. i should have shown her s something . but i never did. i should have had some understanding of her fear and rejection and sadness.

my grandmother had a voice like a dragon.

she always had smoke pouring out of her mouth. her face twisted in fear almost always. in every photo she looks like someone just burnt her with a lighter. for nearly forty years she couldn't read. the voices in her head never giving her any silence. she took mega doses of sleeping pills at three in the morning. as a child it was great to stay with her. she would bring out trays of greek sugar cookies with almonds and mashed potatoes. apple juice in wine glasses. we would watch hours of tv and stay up as late as i could. more often than not i would fall asleep with a fist full of candy on the couch watching johnny carson. in the mornings the sun would filter in through the plants she coved her window with, her snores loud and unsteady in the next room. i would watch cartoons and wait for her to get up. even so young i knew that her sleep was a rare privilege. when i got older i would sneak wine and scotch from her kitchen counter.

almost every year for christmas she would give me

a copy of this story. i think she was trying to tell

me that if she could help me should would have.

but she just could not. so hear it is.

it was writen by Hans Christian Anderson.

THE LITTLE MATCH GIRL

IT was late on a bitterly cold, snowy, New Year's Eve. A poor little girl was wandering in the dark cold streets; she was bareheaded and barefooted. She certainly had had slippers on when she left home, but they were not much good, for they were so huge. They had last been worn by her mother, and they fell off the poor little girl's feet when she was running across the street to avoid two carriages that were rolling rapidly by. One of the shoes could not be found at all; and the other was picked up by a boy who ran off with it, saying that it would do for a cradle when he had children of his own. So the poor little girl had to go on with her little bare feet, which were red and blue with the cold. She carried a quantity of matches in her old apron, and held a packet of them in her hand. Nobody had bought any of her during all the long day; nobody had even given her a copper. The poor little creature was hungry and perishing with cold, and she looked the picture of misery. The snowflakes fell upon her long yellow hair, which curled so prettily round her face, but she paid no attention to that. Lights were shining from every window, and there was a most delicious odour of roast goose in the streets, for it was New Year's Eve —she could not forget that. She found a corner where one house projected a little beyond the next one, and here she crouched, drawing up her feet under her, but she was colder

157

than ever. She did not dare to go home, for she had not sold any matches, and had not earned a single penny. Her father would beat her, besides it was almost as cold at home as it was here. They only had the roof over them and the wind whistled through it although they stuffed up the biggest cracks with rags and straw. Her little hands were almost dead with cold. Oh, one little match would do some good! Dared she pull one out of the bundle and strike it on the wall to warm her fingers! She pulled one out, " risch," how it spluttered, how it blazed! It burnt with a bright clear flame, just like a little candle when she held her hand round it. It was a very curious candle too. The little girl fancied that she was sitting in front of a big stove with polished brass feet and handles. There was a splendid fire blazing in it and warming her so beautifully, but—what happened—just as she was stretching out her feet to warm them, —the blaze went out, the stove vanished, and she was left sitting with the end of the burnt-out match in her hand. She struck a new one, it burnt, it blazed up, and where the light fell upon the wall, it became transparent like gauze, and she could see right through it into the room. The table was spread with a snowy cloth and pretty china; a roast goose stuffed with apples and prunes was steaming on it. And what was even better, the goose hopped from the dish with the carving knife and fork sticking in his back, and it waddled across the floor. It came right up to the poor child, and then—the match went out, and there was nothing to be seen but the thick black wall.

Again, she lit another. This time she was sitting under a lovely Christmas tree. It was much bigger and more beautifully decorated than the one she had seen when she peeped through the glass doors at the rich merchant's house this very last Christmas. Thousands of lighted candles gleamed upon its branches, and coloured pictures, such as she had seen in the shop windows, looked down to her. The little girl stretched out both her hands towards them—then out went the match. All the Christmas candles rose higher and higher, till she saw that they were only the twinkling stars. One of them fell and made a bright streak of light across the sky. "Some one is dying," thought the little girl; for her old grandmother, the only person who had ever been kind to her, used to say, "When a star falls a soul is going up to God."

Now she struck another match against the wall, and this time it was her grandmother who appeared in the circle of flame. She saw her quite clearly and distinctly, looking so gentle and happy.

"Grandmother!" cried the little creature. "Oh, do take me with you! I know you will vanish when the match goes out; you will vanish like the warm stove, the delicious goose, and the beautiful Christmas tree!"

She hastily struck a whole bundle of matches, because she did so long to keep her grandmother with her. The light of the matches made it as bright as day. Grandmother had never before looked so big or so beautiful. She lifted the little girl up in her arms, and they soared in a halo of light and joy, far, far above the earth, where there was no more cold, no hunger, no pain, for they were with God.

In the cold morning light the poor little girl sat there, in the corner between the houses, with rosy cheeks and a smile on her face—dead. Frozen to death on the last night of the old year. New Year's Day broke on the little body still sitting with the ends of the burnt-out matches in her hand. She must have tried to warm herself, they said. Nobody knew what beautiful visions she had seen, nor in what a halo she had entered with her grandmother upon the glories of the New Year!

while she was dying my stepmother played a tape of enya's watermark album. my grandmother hated enya and my stepmother. it seemed so fucking unfair that she was able to pick the music. she was

so pushy and me and my father and my friend who came along where all to fucking heartbroken to say anything. me and my friend should have sang songs. my dad should have played his guitar. we should have played my grandmother's favorite

songs. she loved romantic music. its sweeping changes and drama. she loved it when my dad played music and sang songs about frying fish and candy men.

her mouth had tubes running into it. tubes in her arm, her chest, her bladder. her skin was pale but there where red sores on her face. her arms thinner and the veins larger than ever before. her breath was mathematical, controlled by a machine. her eyes sunken and blue at the edges. the living dead.

we watched her for a while and had a meeting with the doctors. they all said the same thing. she is going to die. you as the family get to pick the time.

her bowels, her lungs, her heart, her kidneys, her brain and her veins where all broken. any of those alone could kill her, but they all decided to give up at once. we decided to let go. in ten minutes. my father's cousin came and

cried, my father rubbed pacholi oil on her arms and chest. i looked at the ground. and out the window my friend pulled on his shirt sleeve and put his arm around me. the nurse came in and told us to move

to the other side of the curtain so she could take the breathing tube out. the sound was horrible. we came back and she was there. heaving. she would

stop breathing for moment than sit up and gasp.
she sounded like a horse, at once stiff and floppy.
my father started to cry, slow at first then hard. his

face torn with grief. he hugged me. even though i
hate it when he touches me, it felt far too heartless
to not hug him while his mother died before our
very eyes. we watched for about a half an hour and
she was not still. i left. i couldn't take it anymore.

her almost breathing, the oil in the air, my
stepmother's stupid fucking face and her stupid
fucking watermark on auto-reverse. my friend
holding my hand so tight, my fingers twisted. my
housemate came and picked me up and we went
home. when he got back to the house the band that
had played the night before was still there. hanging
out and taking showers. fuckers.

Once when i was in high school my grandmother was watching me while my father was out of town.

My boyfriend came over and we had sex in my bedroom while my grandmother watched simpsons episodes on tv in the living room.

I always thought that no one could hear anything down there, so i didn't feel any pressure to keep quiet.

When we came down stairs she a said, "i hope you use birth control, because you are two young to get pregnant. And that boyfriend of yours is two young to help you. Just be sure you are at least on the pill."

i was 16 and i don't think i had ever been so embarrassed. Not only had she heard us fucking, but that meant that all the other times i had thought i was safe, my dad had been able to hear everything as *he* watched tv every night. For years he just sat there and listened. Sick.

Never had i wanted to kill my father so much.

Once, me and my father took her to Christmas mass at the local catholic church.

It was a midnight mass and when we went to pick her up she was pretty drunk. It appeared that she had drank a two liter bottle of Carlo Rossi blush and some scotch.

She was having trouble walking and kept shouting. I remember being a little scared but it was something i was used too. Once we got to the church my dad was too embarrassed to go inside with her so i did.

She was talking really loud and kept saying that the priest was stupid and not saying the right things. She was really pissed off that the service was in english rather than latin. She was slurring a lot and not making a whole lot of

sense. But even stone cold sober it was hard to understand her sometimes. Every one was staring and i could hardly keep a strait face. The whole thing seemed so funny at the time.

When the part came to kneel and pray she refused, saying that the church was shitty and she wished she was in a real church, like the ones in new york. I stood up with her and gave everyone dirty looks. At one point she tried to light a ▨▨▨▨ but i stopped her. She yelled

at me a little. But nothing to serious. My father came in when everyone around us started singing my grandmother stepped out of the pews and started singing her heart out. Pounding her fist and swaying around.

Her voice gruff and

demanding.

As we left she mumbled

to the priest something

about Latin

My grandmother loved the color blue. One of her favorite hobbies other than crochet, was to refinish chairs. She would get them from the local thrift store, and sand them down. Sometimes it would take a few days with the sandpaper to make her happy. She would paint them any shade of blue she could find. Robin's egg, pale sky, the color of the sea at night, the color of the blood underher skin.

she would paint pretty little flowers all over the back rest or the seat.

Blue bells, tulips, lilacs.

She gave our family new chairs all the time, downstairs Clogged with them. we had to give them away to friends.

CAKES

4½ teaspoons double-acting baking powder
2 teaspoons maple sugar
2 teaspoons salt
Beat the mixture while adding:
2 cups mi...
Add and bare...

OATMEAL

BUCKWHEAT CAKES

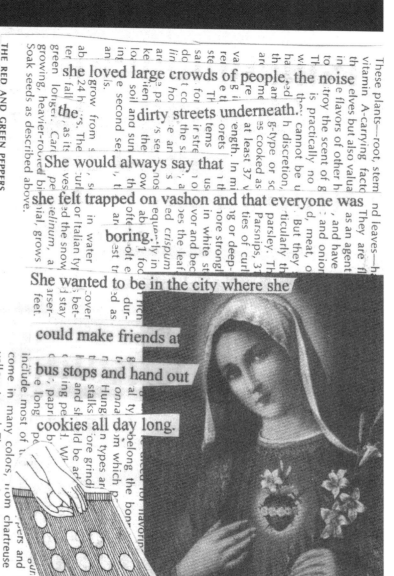

she loved large crowds of people, the noise

the dirty streets underneath.

She would always say that

she felt trapped on vashon and that everyone was

boring.

She wanted to be in the city where she

could make friends at

bus stops and hand out

cookies all day long.

My grandmother always called me her little Cleopatra with my bright eyes and dark dark hair.

She said i looked just like a little elizabath taylor.

And that someday i would rule egypt, or at least hollywood. She often wondered if i would end up as "stacked" as my mother.

More than once she asked if my tits where as big as my oldersister's yet.

I refused to see myself in her, the genes of my father.

She told me that i would have wonderful skin until the day that i died. But i never once thought that i looked like her.

I always wished i looked like my mothers birth mother, someone i had never met.

I hated the idea of my
fathers blood being Near mine.

Near her death, i
looked through a photo album she had and it was
as thought i was looking at pictures of myself in
costume.

Her as a child in the early thirties. Her
with my father as in infant in central park, 1949.
her eyes like mine.

Not yet faded with years of life

and countless pills.

Her mother had been a flapper.

A gin drinking party girl and my grandmother was

born in 1928. there where pictures of my great
grandmother, nana, with a short beaded gown and a
bottle of of something in her hand. 1925.

her drunk
smile so much like mine. I look so much like both
of them.

It took me until i was eighteen years old to
even want to understand where i had come from.

My father so tainted and fucked up that i didn't
even care to understand my family history.

drunk flapper, a crazy beat-nik, my dad a hippy,
and me. Silly punk girl. A wild

It makes me wonder what
sort of amazing wonderful child i will have.

I Love a grand-Mother
her name is Nancy.
X She Lets me stay
up Late! I Love

Hey!
. carrie

This is a note from
my older sister
that i found in my
grandmother's cook book.

A few days after her death i was sleeping over at her house.

Me and her sister had watched a movie and ate what was left of my grandmother's food. We drank the last of her wine and went to sleep. I was on the couch with a thin afghan. Sometime in the night i woke up to a stearn horse voice whispering "wake up, hey, wake up. I turned over and it was my grandmother. She was wearing her favorite blue suit jacket and her long gold necklace with the flower pendent. Her hair was brushed back and her nails where clean.

She looked me right in the eye and said, "don't worry about me anymore. I will be ok. I'll be fine. I love you. Good bye." and then she was gone.

I never thought i would miss her at all.

I first noticed her absence during christmas, when the tin of smoky cookies didn't come in the mail, and i did not get a card. The silly second hand card with mary on it.

The following birthday was when it really hit me. I did love her, even though i never knew it. Our birthdays are two days apart, and while she was alive we would have joint dinners and give each other blue gifts. It was always strained but nice in it's own way.

I spend so much time being angry that i never took the time to care for her.

As the time goes by i miss her more and more. i find myself thinking about her, her life, the stores i missed out on. I wish i could talk to her and tell her thank you.

recently as the early 1950s sights
d sounds in even the best mental
spital could be harrowing—the vio-
it patients kept under restraint by
aps or bed sheets; seriously dis-
rbed psychotics yelling in mental
rment; others huddled in frozen si-
ace.

This
time it was her grandmother who appeared in the
circle of flame.

i still have back issues of number one,
it is writings about
incest.

number two is about homes
i have lived in.

they are $1 and two stamps.

i also have a short one shot that
is a collection of letters called

dear step dad, it's
one stamp.

neely bat chestnut

6653 carlton ave s

seattle wa 98108

p.s. Her name was Kathrine,
but we always called her nancy.

neely
6653 carleton ave s
seattle wa 98108

mend my dress

number four   Leporiphobia-

fear of rabbits or,

what if little

red ridding

hood saw

a rabbit

instead

of a wolf?

by neely bat chestnut

Lets talk about fear. Fear of rabbits. I am

afraid of rabbits. Very, very very afraid. I am

met with jokes and funny looks when I tell

most people this But rabbits are soo cute

~~some~~ I dont know where it started for i have

always had at least a sight aversion to them,

that aversion has been reinforced through out

the years of my life. Its something i would like

to explain. I want to make it clear that i'm not

fucking joking.

As though it is stupid to fear these things.

These goofy ironic bunnies. I would like to get

to a point where i could see a drawing of a

ONCE upon a time there were four little Rabbits, and
their names were

                        Flopsy,
                        Mopsy,
                        Cotton-Tail,
                        and Peter.

They lived with their mother in a sandbank, underneath the root of a very big fir tree.

rabbit and not be afraid. I think it is crazy to

think that i would ever *like* rabbits, but i want

to get my fear in check. So I am writing this

zine as a way to better understand my fear

and gain control over it. Tracing Some of

memories. And to hopefully help the reader

gain some understanding to the world of a

the art work in this zine is from:
the best word book ever by richard scary,
the joy of cooking, my book house and
the transitive...

phobic person.

When i was six my father gave me a stuffed animal bunny. It was brown with black stripes and golden eyes. It had a white tail and it was about four inches tall. Two little white felt teeth came out of it's mouth. My dad made up a game when the bunny would sit on my shoulder and i had to stay very very still. Pretending not to notice it but always keeping an eye on it. I would be forced to read, or study my math book. Most times i had to practice my spelling homework. He would make me pet it and pretend to like it, but if i really did like it, or he sensed that i trusted it, it would attack me. He would put the rabbit under my chin and on my neck and he would put his other hand between my legs and on my chest. Rubbing hard. Sometimes the rabbit would make sounds. The sounds where low and mean, coming from my fathers neck. Sometimes the rabbit would go up my skirt

Will it be likely to hurt someone?

The soft, furry rabbit makes a gentle and friendly pet.

and make biting sounds. My fathers teeth chomping. It was always scary and i was always on guard. Sometimes i would cry. But i could never show it. To be vulnerable was certain death. I dont remember ever crying out. No voice. I was to scared to make a sound. As if opening my mouth would cause the rabbit to crawl down my throat and into my heart.

Snowshoe Rabbit
(Winter)

Rabbits

Snowshoe Rabbit
(Summer)

Turning me into the horrible beast. On the nights where it didn't touch me, the brown rabbit lived on top of the book shelves always watching when my father would touch me while i studied my homework or watched movies.. It was always looking, and never to be trusted. I believed that it would come to life at night and find me if i was bad. Maybe my father told me that, but i dont remember.

Around the

same time my mother rented a copy of watership down and

i watched it. The rabbits in it eat each other alive and they

are mean. I don't remeber much of what happens, i just

remember being scared. When i think of rabbits i am filled

with the image of them tearing themselves apart. I know

that if they had the chance they would get me inserted.

When i was twenty, my friend told me i really should read

watership down, that it was there favorite book. I was madly

in love with this friend. I tried, i paper clipped a bit of

colored paper over the book cover. (i was afraid the rabbit

on the cover would bite my fingers as i read) i could only get

one paragraph into it before i started shaking and sweating

and i could not catch my breath The friend was

disappointed that i didnt read it, and i dont think he ever

believed that i even tried.

At age 18 i had a dream about a black bunny. In the dream i was driving to my best friends house, i pulled into the yard and began walking across the it. Just then a bunny, the size of a large dog came hopping up to me. I tried to act unafraid and the bunny stopped and started eating the grass. Running away the bunny pounced and begin eating my leg, tearing the meat off, exposing the bones and tendons. I was forced to stay totally still and then the bunny would hop away. this went on for sometime. I awoke covered in sweat.

DOMESTICATED RABBITS

Belgian Hare

Himalayan Rabbit

A few weeks ago, i was looking in a catalog at clothing, and i came across a shirt with a rabbit printed on the front, a brown and white spotted one. I was struck with the urge to buy it. To buy it and store it away for some future where i am no longer afraid. For when i have concerred this and moved on. A badge to wear to show myself that i am stronger than anything i have been trained. I did not end up buying it. I can not see and end to this. I am not willing to give it up.

Down they came fluttering, one and all;
Over the brown fields they danced and flew,
Singi   rabbit   new.
"Cri   ds so long,
Littl   ong;
Say
Ah   know."
Dan   ves went,
Wi   ere content;
Soon, fast asleep in their earthy beds,
The snow laid a coverlid over their heads.

I worry that someday i will have a little child and they will want to get a pet, or they will have one in the class room at school. I could see myself not wanting to touch my child with out first giving them a hot bath, supper hard scrubbing new clothes and i would want them to tell me that they hate rabbits. I would make them promise that they would never touch them. Ever. I would not want any books in the house that had photos, or any stories with rabbits in them. No clothing with rabbits printed on them. All of this adds up to abuse on my part, but i dont know how to stop these feelings. I dont know how to calm down and i don't know if i even want to. It just seems better to not have children at all. I know that this is not right, and when i am feeling better i know that it's all nonsense, that it would only hurt my child. And that thinking about it all now, before having a baby is the best thing to do. How do i stop these feelings? This need for control?

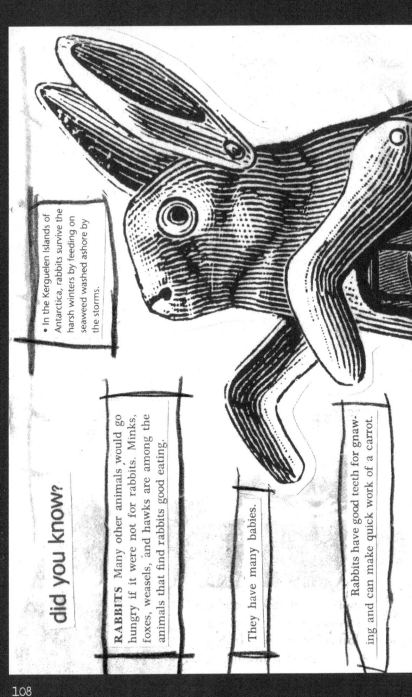

did you know?

RABBITS Many other animals would go hungry if it were not for rabbits. Minks, foxes, weasels, and hawks are among the animals that find rabbits good eating.

They have many babies.

Rabbits have good teeth for gnawing and can make quick work of a carrot.

• In the Kerguelen Islands of Antarctica, rabbits survive the harsh winters by feeding on seaweed washed ashore by the storms.

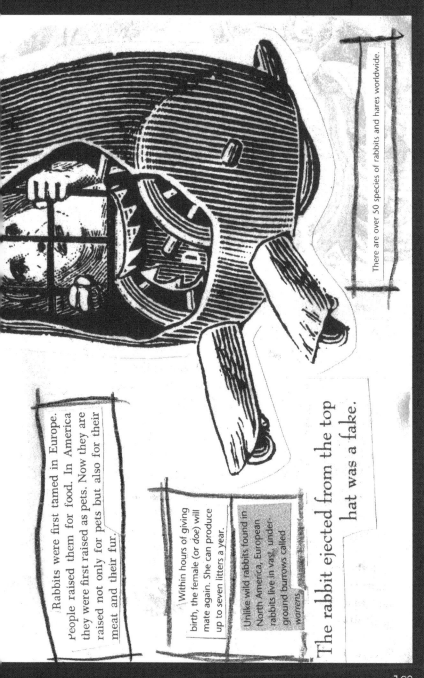

There are over 50 species of rabbits and hares worldwide.

Rabbits were first tamed in Europe. People raised them for food. In America they were first raised as pets. Now they are raised not only for pets but also for their meat and their fur.

Within hours of giving birth, the female (or *doe*) will mate again. She can produce up to seven litters a year.

Unlike wild rabbits found in North America, European rabbits live in vast, underground burrows called *warrens*.

The rabbit ejected from the top hat was a fake.

A Song for Easter

When i was young i hated easter, well thats not fully true. I love hunting for eggs. All day long i would beg my father to re hide them. All over the house. in the back yard, the front yard. I would find them in my socks, behind the books in there shelves, in the trees, under the holly bush, in my fathers tool box. It was so fun. I would beg and plead over and over again. Pulling on his hand, My father would give in until the sky's where dark and it was past my bedtime. I always found them, a little hound dog. I never lost one.

What i really hated was the night before. Despertly trying to fall asleep i would imagine over and over all the different ways the easter bunny could look. Would it be a tall human like monster with merely a bunny head? Perhaps wearing a waistcoat like the one in alice in wonderland? Would it be waist high with a magic floating basket drifting along side it?

All through snows of winter
You've been fast asleep!
Sunshine now is calling;
Little rabbits leap!

Would it be more than one bunny Two, three? Could it be a family of rabbits, all of them holding one egg in there mouths? Would it be a normal sized one? With it's quiet hunting eye. A perfectly normal looking rabbit with its secrets hidden away. I was so scared of all of them.

Knowing that it would come in to the house, by magical means, it could even get into my bedroom with out my permission and watch me as i slept. They could even put things under my pillow, like the dark chocolates i would find, or the fleece carrots. What else did they do? Where else did they touch me? And why was a supposed to be excited about this? Fear fear fear.

Peter Rabbit

this was clipped from
life magazine 1952

Although few rabbits live more than eight years, this is Peter Rabbit's 50th birthday, and he is as lively as ever. In 1902 Peter first appeared in public print in a tiny book written and illustrated by Beatrix Potter. As a child Beatrix had not been permitted to go to school by her wealthy, austere Victorian father. She studied under tutors and played by herself with dolls. But in the summer the family usually went to England's Lake District and there Beatrix, a shy but imaginative girl, first discovered her half-real, half-poetic world of rabbits and chipmunks, ponds and marshes.

Beatrix acquired a live pet rabbit, called *Benjamin Bunny* (*above*). After Benjamin died she got another—and named him Peter. Then, when Noel Moore, 5-year-old son of her German teacher, became ill, she wrote him a story about "Peter Rabbit" and drew pictures to go with it (*below*). Noel loved it, and his delight encouraged Beatrix to expand the story into a book. *The Tale of Peter Rabbit* was rejected by six publishers before it was finally printed in 1902 by Warne & Co.

A lonely spinster of 36, Beatrix fell in love with her publisher, Norman Warne. But before they could be married—against her father's wishes—Warne died. During the next 10 years, sad and dejected, Beatrix continued to write children's books. In 1913, at 47, she married William Heelis, and her literary creativeness came to an end. But the fame of Peter Rabbit continued to spread. In the U.S. *The Tale of Peter* outsold all her other books by four to one. By the time of her death in 1943 the book had been translated into five languages, had sold several million copies and Peter Rabbit had become the most loved animal in all the world.

BEATRIX POTTER'S FAMOUS COTTONTAIL

PETER APPEARED LIKE THIS IN FIRST BOOK

BENJAMIN WAS PHOTOGRAPHED BY AUTHOR

FAMOUS LETTER to Noel Moore, retrieved by Beatrix, was expanded into book. In book Mrs. Rabbit warns children

to stay away from Farmer McGregor's garden: "Your Father had an accident there; he was put in a pie by Mrs. McGregor."

BEATRIX was 38 when photo was taken, two years after book appeared.

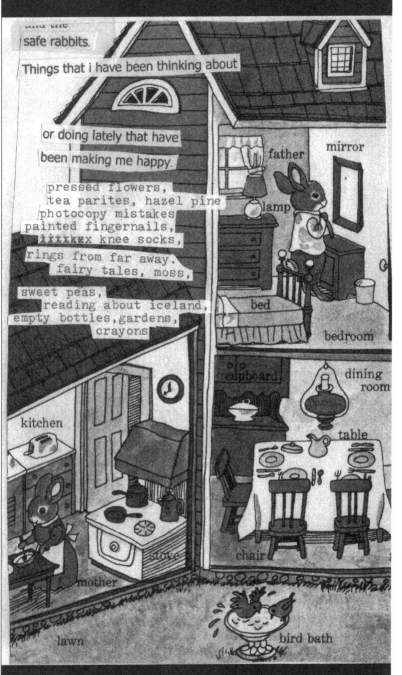

and the
safe rabbits.

Things that i have been thinking about

or doing lately that have
been making me happy.

pressed flowers,
tea parites, hazel pine
photocopy mistakes
painted fingernails,
littkex knee socks,
rings from far away.
fairy tales, moss,

sweet peas,
reading about iceland,
empty bottles,gardens,
crayons

father

mirror

lamp

bed

bedroom

cupboard

dining
room

kitchen

table

stove

chair

mother

lawn

bird bath

i guess i should say that i dont hate *all* rabbits. I love peter rabbit, and the velveteen rabbit, and the rabbits in Richard scary books. They dont make me unconvertible. I feel just fine. I even like them. Its so strange to have some level of comfort with these creatures like i can see a time when maybe i would not be scared of any of them, but most of the time, that idea seems just silly. I can almost understand why more normal people would like them, they jump, have soft fur, maybe never like to be petted. But the bottom line is, they fucking eat there babies. When my fathers house burnt down, most of my books and toys where ruined, but

the stuffed rabbit, high on the top shelve was mostly safe. His right paw a little melted. His fur was short and stiff, melted in the high heat of the blaze. His eyes had begun to boil. Little bubbles made it look almost like glitter. I kept him for years. I dont know why. Something about seeing him ruined, melted and blind made me feel better, stronger somehow. Like i had won.

Do i need this?

The good side of this fear:

i have a concrete way to

funnel

all this panic and

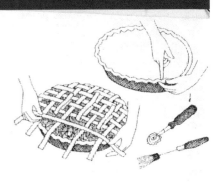

distrust and anger at my father into something that is easy to avoid. These rabbits don't get hurt

feelings when i dont look at them, they dont care if i have

to hide photographs of them. Its really ok to never pet one

or want a shirt with them printed on it. Its ok to never read

watership down or give a copy of the runaway bunny to my

children. All of this is ok. So why do i feel like i need to get

ride of this phobia? To take control? To fully hold my father

accountable? To make sure that i never
am the perpetrator?

To stop blaming those little soft eared creatures for my

fucked up emotional state? Maybe its all of these things.
Right now i can not decide where to go. I dont know what

the right choice is. Do i confront my father and tell him how

his touching and puppetry has ruined me? To i tell him to

be sorry for what he has done? How would my life be if i

didnt have this over my head?

Thank you Cathrine,

thank you for reading. As with most zine writers, i love mail, so please write and tell me what you think.

back copies of my zine are always going to be made

as of now, my address is 6653 carlton ave s seattle wa 98108

number three is about my grandmother,

number two is about houses,

issue number one is writings about incest,

these are all $2 and two stamps.

i have a one shot that is a collections of

letters to the different stepfathers i have had,

this one is just a stamp.

Trades are welcome

Dewey Cottontail

You can f me on livejournal,

under kinderdoll

email me, neely_ohara@hellokitty.com

dig

read

Flopsy, Mopsy, and Cotton-Tail, who were good little bunnies, went down the lane to gather blackberries; but Peter, who was very naughty, ran straight away to Mr. McGregor's garden, and squeezed under the gate!

118

Grit & Glitter

A duet on femme identity by

Neely Bat Chestnut
and
Hazel Pine

Neely

As i wrote this, it became very clear to me
that being femme is a big fuck you to my
father, to my brother. By being femme,
i am getting back me girlhood, my womanhood
that they stole. I am saying fuck you
for making me feel weak and like I was bad.
Fuck you, I'm going to drink tea and cook
meals, i'm going to wear skirts every fucking

day and i'm going to love it.

Fuck you world, I am femme.

HELLO HELLO

Hello. My name is Neely
Bat Chestnut. I am 24 I
I was born female, I
identify as queer. I am

in a long term

relationship with a male
bodied man. I am white,

my early life was middle
class, and my later child
-hood was more lower class
I have gone to some college
and I have been into punk
for 12 years.

it's nice to meet you.

please write or email with any feedback:

6653 Carleton ave S
seattle, wa
98108

neely_ohara@hellokitty.com

HOW DO FEMME

Neely

For me, femme my femme identity is something that i hold dear and something that hankers back to a false idea of my own chldhood. Playing dress-up and going on teddy bear

picnics. I dress like I have no one to tell me what to do, and that includes ending up wearing clothes intended for girls 20

years younger. I have a deep love of peter

pan collars and lace. Knee socks, fake pearls and every color of the rainbow. Doll houses and something else I cannot quite place. It doesn't always work right because I don't do

a lot of the things that society tells us is "right" for a woman of my age, make-up, shaved skin and being nice. But really i am

nice, just not in the "right ways". Most of the time I feel as thought I am this stranger outsider in the world of women. It's

ribbons   cake

YOU DEFINE

as though I never "grew into a woman" when i started to bleed or decided i wanted to have children. I don't really fit. As a

punk, it works. But when I go to the Anna Sui counter to buy eyeshadow, i always feel a little disconnected. No, I will not feel

like i need a sexual partner to feel like a valid adult. i call myself femme because it fits the best. I do like "girl" things, but maybe not womanly things. Most of my habits would make my grandmother proud. Sewing, baking and art. I love to cook large meals

for people, I love to take tea with honey and lay around in my handmade clothes and day dream about braids and ribbons and names

for my child. I love to curl my eyelashes and to paint my nails and god how i wish i could have been a ballerina. I call myself femme not because these things make me weak, but because they make me strong. For me femme is about taking all of my gender learning,

thinking about it long and hard and taking the bits back that work for me. The things

that feel right and forgetting the rest.

necklace  crown

Neely

I remember being about five, and my mother
forcing me into a purple jumper. I fucking
hated that thing. It had been a gift
from some family member and it was very
important that I wear it.

my mother was pulling it over my head and
I was screaming. She yelled and yelled and I
kicked her. The jumper was mashed over my
head and she walked out. Like she had

won the great battle. I pulled the jumper
over my head, took my scissors and cut it
right from the bottom of the last ruffle to
the top near the first button. Put on my

pants, my blue t-shirt and with the
jumper balled up in my fists, walked
down the stairs, I dropped it
at my mother's feet and sat down at
the kitchen table.

GENDER ROLES

What I remember most about this was that I felt naked with the skirt on. Only tights to protect me It wasn't that I hated the jumper, or dresses. It was that I felt far too exposed. Ripe for the picking.

I needed to wear skirts to make everyone happy, because they were so pretty it never even mattered if I was unhappy. It was never discussed. My body was only for other people to enjoy.

♡ Femme

eloise

kathleen hanna

Matt

Tara

Daniell

Joan Nestle

marilyn monroe

dorothy gale

Heroes ♡

tilda Bernstein Sycamore

pj harvey

a Hardy

le Warhola

courtney love

Neely

My father was always very vocal about his hatred for boys. There is a picture of my

mother, my two sisters and me all nude in a bath tub. Growing up, my father always called this photo "lady soup". He would refer to us as his babes. Later after he moved out he would always say, "I'm glad you are a girl, so I can live in a house full of hot babes."

Never mind that I was five and never mind that he didn't live with anyone else.

To be female was to be a victim, to be a sex plaything for my father. Something that was weak. Afraid. Sexy. To be a girl was to be

just like my father wanted. Daddy's little

girl, as they say.

CONTINUED ON NEXT PAGE

13

When I was a little girl, I decided that
didn't want to be friends with other little
girls, i enjoyed the company of boys so much
more. Maybe by being friends with boys, my

father would forget that I was a girl. Maybe
he would stop touching me, maybe he would

just hate me and forget about me. The boys
in my neighborhood seemed better somehow. Me
and my best friend played in the woods and
got stung by bees. We snuck into people's
houses and watched movies.
It was fun.

When I was in middleschool I learned about
punk rock and most of the punks I knew were
scrappy looking boys or girls that looked and
acted tough, shoplifting and drinking all the
time. Punk To be femme was to be "normal" to
be a preppy or wanna-be prom queen. To be any
anything but boyish was not punk rock. All
rules of girlhood were thrown out. Girls were

girls were equal to boys
as long as we acted like them

HOW DO YOU INDENTIFY AS PUNK + FEMME

Neely

Two words. Riot Grrrl. Even reading the issues
of Seventeen magazine with its silly write x up
about riot grrl. Getting it all wrong.
Only I didn't know at the time. I was
13 and sitting in science class. Most of
the article was about how they dressed.
The girl with the hello kitty band-aids,
the other girl with the barbie t-shirt
and where written on her arm. Reading
the book Girl Power by Hillary Carlip and
the chapter about riot grrrl.. These
amazing amazing smart strong girls, readir

    their words and feeling like I could fit
into this world. That there was a huge
network of young women like
myself, writing and reading and going to
shows, calling people on their shit. Maybe
before the spray painting of billboards they,
as a group, watched Cinderella and did each
others make-up. Maybe they had manifestos
tucked into their knee socks. Being in love
and lust with amazing women, being
friends with them, watching them live through
all the shit piled on top of them made me
proud to be a girl. It made me proud to be
fucking tough and to not reject the fact that
I was a girl.

maidens act flattered. They all primp: smooth their hair, brush their clo
their curls, put on lipstick, etc.

March 2007

mend my dress

#5

girl love, girl revolution.

stories of friendship.

by neely bat chestnut.

i am sitting in the sun, the first warm day of spring. i've got a blue eye crayon around my eyes and big white sunglasses on. typing on my new computer, i feel like a fashion magazine.

i want to write a zine about being a girl. a girl growing up in a hateful world, in a sad school, with my sadder friends.

i want to write about scuba school, with the wonders of water and time and air. i want to write

april 2007

bikini kill broke up, rape and harassment did not magically dissolve about love and raindrops and heartshaped cookies and striped socks and revolution.

few weeks ago, me and my friends went on tour. two read from a zine on femme identity, and two played magical music. we burned candles and sang songs in the car, we got drunk and some of us kissed strangers at a queer prom. we became closer and i think we made some good memories. memories i hope to take with me. i want to hold on

to them, and my friends forever. when i think of these girls, i am reminded of old friendships past and the love i felt for those people.

I LOVE YOU!

times when we would hold hands and promise to never give up. here are some stories about love.

i chose only to write about people i am no longer friends with, it seemed better, less messy somehow. i also didn't write about every girl that had a huge impact on me, of course, this is just a few. love, neely

♡Ullelee♡

we where in kindergarten together. ms. dunn, room number one at wilkes elementary. she was new, her family had just come back from year long trip around the world in their boat. sailing the seven seas, this little five year old seemed like the smartest person i had ever met. they lived across the bay from me, on a tiny island called treasure island. it had a two room log cabin and a very small dock. to get to the house me and my sister would have to row across the bay on a tiny dingy.

her house was full.

the oldest of six. her and her siblings would sleep on little bunk beds, five tiny beds in a row, the youngest in bed with mom and dad, or sleeping in the smallest crib on the floor. mom and dad slept in a lovely bed right next to the fire place, in the living room.

i wanted her mother to take notice of me, and decide that i was good enough to be one of the family. i thought i could just be another set of hands to help her mother and father with all the babies.

if they just liked me enough.

i could even sleep on the tiny porch. the bathroom the most fun, ullelee and i would take baths there, singing mermaid songs and washing each other's hair. in the summertime we would play in the sand, making up stories about pirates, fairies and witches. at school she would be made fun, her wild family, her weird hippy name, but most of all, for being my friend. she wore nice jeans and had pretty dark blond hair. sometimes her nails would be painted the lightest of pink and she was my hero.

i wanted to travel in my grandfather's sailboat to china, across the world. i wanted parents that would let me do anything, so long as i was safe. i wanted to not have a tv, only books and craft supplies. i wanted a father who would joke and laugh and be helpful, and who would tell stories about working in new zealand, and india. a mother who would bake bread and tell us how little girls in africa dressed. me and ullelee took gymnastics together, her legs working in ways that mine never would. i was made fun of for being the fattest in class. the other girls didn't want to get dressed at the same time as me, for my fat was contagious. ullelee would wait with me, and we would get dressed alone, no matter how many times the teacher yelled at us for being late.

she would hold my hand as we walked to the mats. she was always kind to me, and never made me feel bad. she was the first person in my life to do that.

or at least the first i remember.

i don't remember why we stopped being friends, maybe i became jealous and threatened to crush her with my desperate six year old love. the last i heard about her, my mother told me she was working as a stripper in thailand, and was doing lots of heroin.

i have know way of knowing if that is true. i hope where ever she is, she is happy.

in second grade my love was with a pretty smart girl named chelsea she had short blond hair and a pretty house. at recess we would play in the huge tires or in the small stream that ran alongside the school yard. she could do the best tricks on the

Chelsea

monkey bars. she smelled like watermelon shampoo and dirt. she had soft brown eyes and she could run way faster than me. she never showed off. i fell in love with her as hard as a second grade girl can. i thought of her while i waited for the school bus in the morning, wondering what she would be wearing that day, the horror of, "what if she is sick?" i thought of her at dinner, i wanted to know what she was doing. was she thinking of me?

i wrote her little notes, and she always had to ask me what they said, my hand writing was so bad. we where in girl scouts together, and that gave us two

extra hours a week to spend time together. we went on camping trips and i told her stories about my trip to new york. we would gather leaves and talk about getting old and what type of house we would have. we would talk about how it must be cool to be grown up.

we played house. she was always the wife, and i the dad that did not work. at one point, she started playing with another girl at recess, a name i can no longer recall. i was fucking mad with jealousy. my heart was so broken. i cried all recess, i told the other girl i was going to kill her, i think i even cut my hair i was so sad. i told my mom i hated her. i begged her to play only with me. i told her that no way could she be my friend and this other girls friend at the same time. didn't she know that i needed her? and i think she made the right choice. she ditched me. how could she not?

alison

while i was in kindergarten my father lived with a nice lady. Her granddaughter was three years younger than me, but she was so fun and smart. she came over almost every weekend i came to visit. the days with out her slow and boring. we played in the woods and made forts in the living room. card table and lace curtains. we would lay in our nests all day, drawing on the underside of the table with

crayons and drawing on our bodies in magic marker. There was a large cedar bathtub in the bathroom, and me and Alison would take baths together there. pretending we where pond dwelling mermaids. we watched charlotte's web over and over. i would cry almost every time. i always worried that i was being mean. while she was

around, i believed that my father would not hurt me. alison, my protector. there was a rope swing in the yard, under a great wide tree. in the spring the pretty green leaves made a curtain. the summer and was a shield from the hot sun, the fall, a crunchy blanket to crash into. crinkling under our

tiny weights. in the winter time, the low sloping hill beneath the bare tree was just right for sledding. we spent a lot of time under that tree. making up stories and loving our days together. While i was in fourth grade, my father moved out of the house, and cut the friendship short.

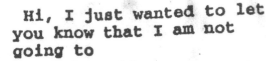

Excuse Me

Hi, I just wanted to let you know that I am not going to

★ smile

★ act dumb

★ hide my body

★ pretend

★ lie

★ be silent

for you. And that everything I do I do for me and I'm not going to let you laugh at me, make fun of me, harrass me, abuse me or rape me anymore. Because I am a girl and me and my girlfriends are not afraid of you!

Riot grrrl? In 2007? fuck yes.

riot grrrl is still valid. 100%. incest didn't just go away when bikini kill broke up, rape and harassment did not magically dissolve when the spice girls hit top 40. there is still a need for punk rock feminism at nearly every single punk show. shows at "friends" houses where my girlfriend got dragged to the floor by her hair by some blacked out drunk dude. everyone just

laughed. there is still a need for it in every response to my zines i get from some girl across the country who tells me about her grandpa raping her. there is still a need for it in every every time i hear my friends tell me how stupid they are. there is a need for it every time i wait for the bus and some man asks me to get in his car. our government is shutting out birth control, stamping out abortion rights, we need direct action, and we need safe

spaces for the girls and women of our scenes. Riot grrrl is not the end of feminism, it's a basic starting point. There are always new girls and women who will need something basic like the phrase girl love, or the simple idea that we don't need to be fighting each other.

That unity and support are some of the most important things in the world.

Michelle

i thought she was perfect. she had come from the east coast with her sister, Sarah, who i also was super good friends with. they showed up at my middle school half way though the year. i thought that Michelle was a boy, with her man pants and short hair. her way of not talking to anyone. i thought she was hot. we became friends in the gym locker room, we the only two girls that would get naked. she was almost punk, fucking tough and wore little baby clips in her hair. she was

short and fat like me, we could share bras and underwear and socks and hair pins and we would take baths together. run around her house naked, screaming bikini kill lyrics. "why can't, why can't, why can't i cum!!..." we both where learning more about riot grrrl, thanks to our friend colleen. we where also both in love with marilyn manson as well. Michelle would make little hand sew dolls of the band members. we would go to grannies attic, the only thrift store on

vashon, and buy anything we thought was glamorous. old prom dresses from the 1980's, slip skirts from the 1960's, purses meant for five year olds, my little ponies, girl scout shirts, fake pearls. it was amazing to have a friend who never once said i was stupid, who seemed to understand me as much as she did. i wanted to be her, and in turn, i wanted her to be me. we would walk to the candy store, holding hands, singing at the top of our lungs..."she is me, i am her. i want to kill her, but it might kill me." we watched jenny ones on v and talked about how fucked up it was that no one seemed to notice how amazing the punk rock goth girls looked

before there makeovers. we wrote fuck you on pale pink slip dresses and got into fights with boys at school. she punched boys who made fun of her and we talked about rape and abuse. i was her first kiss, in the ball pool of the pizza place. we where wrestling and giggling and she burst out that she had never been kissed. with her permission and put my hand on the side of her face

and kissed her with all the love i could muster. with her i thought we would take over the world and spread girl-love everywhere. we would save everyone, and in turn save ourselves. i thought we would friends forever. we where wrong, but it doesn't mater. and it doesn't matter how we became not-friends. what matters is those few years where fucking awesome. and i hope she thinks of me.

part Courtney Love, part Strawberry Shortcake, and always a totally colorful mess.

sarah

she moved from rhoad island, with her sister
michelle. she had long red hair and guns and roses
written in black sharpie on her red converse all
stars. she told me of her speed addiction back

home in road island. she thought that her mom
moved to get her away from the people selling her
drugs. we where in eighth grade. on my birthday, i
went to her house after school, and her mom was
defrosting a chicken in a pan of water on the

counter. it was blue and hard and looking at it, i
decided to never eat meat again. it was thought me
that sarah (and her sister) found out about punk. i
made her tapes of the dead kennedy's of fear and
the lunachicks. we went to shows together.

michelle didn't like shows that much, i think they
where overwhelming for her. sarah and i went
about twice a week. we would take the ferry into
settle and stay out all hours drinking and having a
good time. somehow we never got in trouble for
being late. somehow we always made it back to the

2:00 ferry to Vashon her mother always right there to pick us up at 2:20 in the morning. the first time i did speed was with her. i had bought it from my boyfriend and we took it right before we went to the bikini kill show. sarah, michelle and i in the

sleep

front, getting our bodies mashed together. singing the words we knew, and crying during the ones we didn't. we where so happy. she taught me how to use a curling iron, and i taught her how to sew. we made mini skirts out of sheets and striped t-shirts.

we wore black eye make up and totally ruled the library at school. we worked it out so we had all of our classes together freshman year, so we did not have to be apart and alone in the big world of high school. we would ditch class and go to the woods and drink, she would smoke and we would talk

about how great life would be if only we where older. it was with her that i come into my own with punk rock. before her i wanted to be cool, and with her i just was. it was great.

grade school was a hard time for me. my father was raping me often, my mother was doing lots of

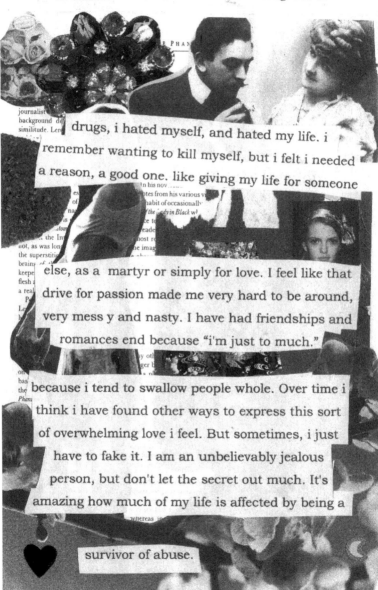

drugs, i hated myself, and hated my life. i remember wanting to kill myself, but i felt i needed a reason, a good one. like giving my life for someone else, as a martyr or simply for love. I feel like that drive for passion made me very hard to be around, very mess y and nasty. I have had friendships and romances end because "i'm just to much."

because i tend to swallow people whole. Over time i think i have found other ways to express this sort of overwhelming love i feel. But sometimes, i just have to fake it. I am an unbelievably jealous person, but don't let the secret out much. It's amazing how much of my life is affected by being a

survivor of abuse.

Things i have been swooning over lately:::
cherry trees, zine tour, marie antonette, crayons, color
photo copies, the new tiny zine library in my house, the
color sea foam, braids.

I have back issues of my zine, and i love trades.

Please write me and tell me what you think of my zine.

jam with

running

little la   if you like, you can find me on livejournal.

wings.   i'm kinderdoll

great fe

in their   Tell me anything. Thank you for reading.

green

stick candies an

pink - and - w

striped stick c

and the choc   6653 Carleton ave s.

and other good

began to dance   seattle wa 98108

brown coffee-

from Java, and

nified tea leaves from   neely_ohara@hellokitty.com

China, joined in th

merrymaking.

neely bat chestnut
6653 carleton ave s.
seattle wa 98108

Mend my Dress zines.

number one.

writing about incest.

number two.

homes i have lived in

number three. the Little Match Girl.

or my dead grandmother.

Number four.

Leporiphobia.

fear of rabbits.

These are all two dollars by mail. or trade

Oxox- neely bat chestnut
6653 carelton ave s.
Seattle wa 98108

mend my dress

number six bathed in blood :

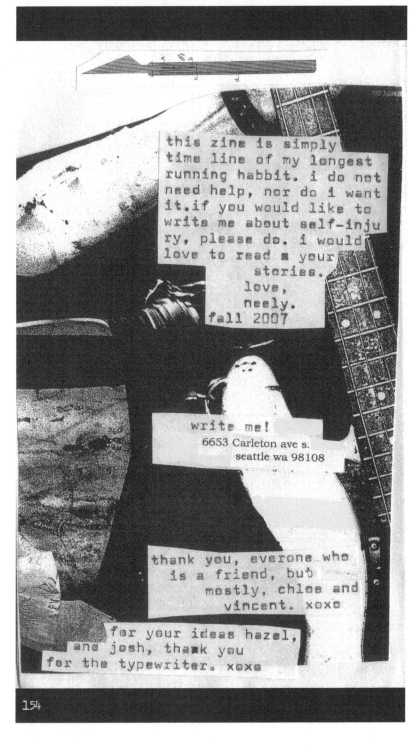

this zine is simply
time line of my longest
running habbit. i do not
need help, nor do i want
it.if you would like to
write me about self-inju
ry, please do. i would
love to read a your
        stories.
        love,
        neely.
fall 2007

write me!
6653 Carleton ave s.
seattle wa 98108

thank you, everone who
is a friend, but
    mostly, chloe and
    vincent. xoxo

for your ideas hazel,
and josh, thank you
for the typewriter. xoxo

154

as i have noted in other zines,
my grandmother was a catholic.
her walls where covered with
paintings of jesus.

Virginal milk, tender breast.
White wings, chaste dove, seraphic lyre.
Tears, sweet exile, brave warrior, little shepherd girl.
Lamb. Lily. Daisy. Rose.

Burning arrow, burn me away until nothing is left.

Saint Thérèse of Lisieux

bleeding heart helpless and
pure.wound wounds where something
that set one free. a ticket to
heavon. the pain was real, but
never something avoid.my grandmo
ther prayed to saints. St. jude,
who was beaten to death with a
club. St. francis, who after a
life of beatings, starvation and
rejection was given the stigmata.

blood flowing from holy cuts.
suffering great pain for his love
of a god.

i was told these things as
a young girl. i was told i was
bad. not always directly. good girls
pray, bad girls don't. godd girls
go to heaven. bad girls, hell.

kx bad girls are worthless.
bad things happen to bad girls.

is it really a suprize that ix
started to cut myself in middle
school? i think not.
the real suprize is that more of
you did not.

so here,
in this little zine igive a story
of cutting, burning, shame, lust,
holy intervention, and something
more

in seventh grade i feel inlove
with a wonderful girl. she had white
eyelashes and a barking laugh. wh -
we held hands and kissed between

classes. wrote letters and called
eachother names. father seaman.
black market rape baby. being in
seventh grade, i was terrible at
expressing any sort of emotion beyond
i love you, i don't want to fight.

even spitting out the words *i'm
sorry* was mostly impossible. i didn't
know x how to tell her i loved her
with words one day after yelling at her
so i cut her name in messy block
letters into the thin skin of my chest
now i can't recall doing the cutting,

but clearly now, i can see the look
on her pretty face. she took me in
her arms and said thank you, she
forgave me. and even though my teeshirt
stuck and pulled at my wounds, even if
everyone else gave me dirty looks, i
did not regret it.
*****

i had a friend in art class the
same year. he wowld cut his arms with
the pointy compas durning talks about
shadding and light. under the desk,
he would pull up his shirt sleeve
and write things xix like, 'fuck life'

SLAYER

666

NIN

'kill me' into his flesh. i would
understand that there was no way out.
no freedom, and nothing to hope for.
no one cared about us.
        not for who ▰▰▰ we where, anyway

i lived with my father because
i was given a choice. him, or
my mother. both where shit, but
at least with my father i could
pick my own clothes.

i was in
love with a girl who had been raped
i did not know who to treat
her well. not at all. nearly all of
our friends had been raped, we
had all be asulted as children.

we didn't know how to act in
our newly sexual bodies.

i felt like a time bomb.

i had a friend,

our friend ship ✦ was purely
based on learning about punk
rock and hurting ourselves.

me and her

would sit up in her loft bed
  listening to black flag, and we
would cut

                    together. once we
decided to take turns on each
other. her favorite way to cause
pain was to scratch the skin
away. she took my hand in her
lap, turned up the first four

years casset. and pulled her finge
  fingers up and down my outter
  forarm. it didn;t bleed, but
the layers of skin fell away
  to the bed, and worked there way
under her dirty fingernaids. i
was left with a pond of white
  blood cells and a new hot pain.

it took weeks to heal.

i think we thought it was all
  very sexy and very punk.

later in the spring of that
year, i figured out how to snap
the blades out of the razors i
used to shave my legs, it opened
up a whole new world of cutting.

sharp, fast and bloody.

my friend got scared and gave
up on cutting. she had found a
voilent outlet in hardcore.
circle pits, boxing matches.

i needed something else.
something less showy, more
control. i xx started cutting my
arms when i masturbated, or in
my morning shower.

sometimes i
cut the tops of my hands in
history class, art class. the
yellow school bus home. these
where all surface cuts, healing
in a weeks time. my body was
covered in them.

as time went on, i would cut
myself after any fight broke out,
after i forgot to do my homework
when i slept late, a missed bus.
after any unfairness seeming
beyond my control. 'but it's not
faaaiiiiirrrrr!!!'

cut*cut*cut

i would smash glass in my bedroom,
cups, plates, jars, i would use th
the broken bits against my skin.

i loved to watch the blood slowly
rise.it was calming and nice.
it didn8t it didn't hurt, much.
like black berries

i was always walking around bare
foot on the sharp floors.

no one knows how easy it
            could be,
to cut my wrist and let my
            soul free,
i slide the razor down my wrist.
blood trickles down as i held up
            my fist.

  - whorehouse of representatives.

    eighth grade sucked.

  I had problems. cheating
one my girlfriend, my boyfriend
AND the guy i made out wut with
sometimes. drinking at school
almost everyday. i got into fights

        lying to everyone about
something. getting wasted and
giving blowjobs in the park.

  the best part was right before
bed. i would cut myself and go
to sleep. everthing was such
  chaos, and bleeding was calm
and all mine.

life went on like this
for awhile. then in my third
year of highschool, i got into
an abusive romantic relationship.

the first few months where
great. he came over after school
and we would watch the trinidy
network.

we would watch
the plasic faced crying womenand
make fun of the sweaty faced men
in suits. sometimes he wanted to
cut me while he fucked me.

sometimes he would not stop.
more than once when i asked, he
slapped me and told me to shut up.

i wrote in my journal,
i miss the times when i was
not afraid of him.

later, he would cry and ask me
why i had made him be so mean.

when i would try to talk to
him about it, the voilence, the
hurt, my sadness he would
act as though nothing had happ
happened. or just say nothing.
a blank look on his face, eyes
looking out the window, or at
his shoes. the worst was when
he called me crazy. other
times, he would acuse me

of having sex with other
people. or of being in love
with someone other than him.
he would tell me he would
kill these people. other time
he would pull out chunks of his
hair. fall at my feet, pulling
at my skirts, begging forgive-
ness.

i wish i could say i
did not enjoy the pathetic
look on his face.

it lasted nearly four years.

me at age 19. really, i was
happy that night.

the last time i cut myself,
myself, in a big way, was over
four years ago. i found out that
a boy had fucked another girl,
while on a date with me. a friend
over heard him say to the other
girl

'i would go down on you, but
i am saving my mouth for my
real girlfriend.'

it was gross, sad, hurtful.
i shut myself in the bathroom
with a razor blade and cut my
upper arm. deeply. i could make
the fat from the lean. i really
should have gotten stiches.

it took nearly four months for
skin to close fully.

the scars are still raised and
some times they itch.

"I won't," smiled Red Riding Hood.

i stopped cutting not because
i wanted to, but because i grew
tired of talking about it. the
worried faces. i grew tired of
people trying to understand, when
they could not, and most of all
i stoped because i was tired of
explaning myself to others.

i like to
picture doing it
again. someday,
when my loved ones

do not think i am
crazy
for wanting a little
bit of my insides on
the outsides.

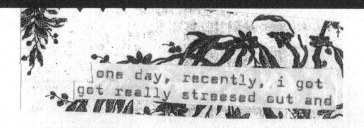

one day, recently, i got
got really streesed out and
mad at myself. i had forgotten
my wallet in mylocker at the
ymca. i had walked five
blocks to the post office,
waited in line twice, then
noticed that i had no money.

i was so frustrated with my
own foolishness. my rage
and selfpitty swelled and i
could think of nothing but
cutting my arms off. i have
not cut myself there in over
four years. i keep myself
from doing it but fanisizing
about it. a huge knife
chopping. slabs of skin
hanging. bones white and blue
underneath.

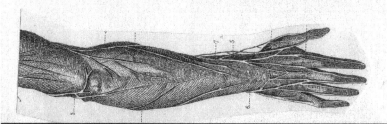

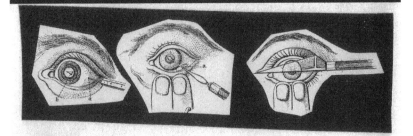

my skin and blood pouring all
over the sidewalk as i made my
way back, retrevibing my sad
x wallet. my heart beats fast as
i imagine the bloodletting. it
excites as well as calms me. i
wanted to cry, but walking through the busness district with
tears my may be one of the most
terrible things in the world.

fancy suits and disoproval from
golden necklaces and red fingers
sensible shoes. cold unemotional
       handbags.

these wounds increasted his
     suffering, but also his grad-
titude to god and his joy.
        -sister loretta claire

i worked in a resturant once,
washing dishes. it was an xxxx easy
job with a nice boss and a speed freak
co-worker. what i hated was that i had
to keep my arms bare for hours on end.
i could not cut my wrists, forearms
or hands. not even my upper arms,
a long time favortie of mine.

i didn't want to talk to my boss about
it, and i certainly did not want bits
of pressed ham in my wounds. dirty
dish water blood. months later, when i
got a new job at a book store, i
celebrated by cutting all these parts
i had missed so much. in the nearly four
years i worked at the book shop i never
once xk wore short sleeves. in the
heat of the summer i had thin long
t-shirts and paper-thin sweaters.

my boss and co-workers never once
said anything. not even when i wore
find fingerless gloves in july to hid
match burns that formed a ring around
my wrist. i thought it was all so
romantic. me, a little starved
bandaged bookshop worker, shelving
in the cold.

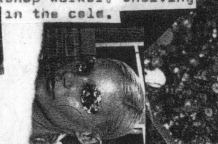

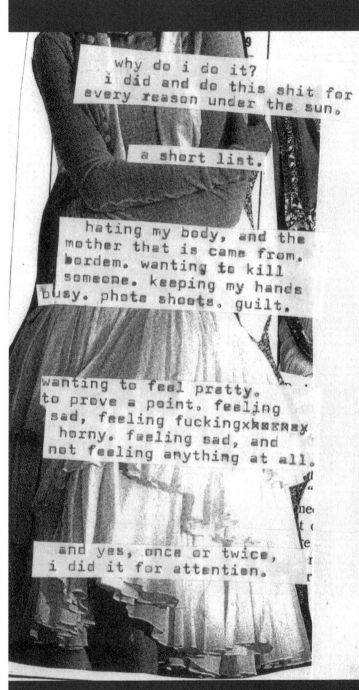

why do i do it?
i did and do this shit for
every reason under the sun.

a short list.

hating my body, and the
mother that is came from.
bordem. wanting to kill
someone. keeping my hands
busy. photo shoots. guilt.

wanting to feel pretty.
to prove a point. feeling
sad, feeling fuckingxⁿⁿⁿ
horny, feeling sad, and
not feeling anything at all.

and yes, once or twice,
i did it for attention.

but for this zine, i feel
like i need to explain myself.

why did i do these things?
in the larger sense. but i dont
know why.

why do it, and others don't?
what makes me diffrent?

what makes one sad girl cut
her wrists, and another simply
cry? i have read all the books
and x none of them have helped
me understand.

Fictional accounts
always seem so hollow, and doctors
are always so insulting.

their simple answers mean
nothing to me.

sometimes, people think the scars
are sexy. as in, i cut my self
so i must like fucking totaly
gross dudes at bars. other times
people think i need help, or some
halfbaked advice about finding my
'innerself'. sometimes, people
feel the need to tell me i am
really fucked up. i've been
screamed at by strangers on the
bus. i once was told that my cuts
could be cool, if only i did

it right. |

i wondered, vaguely, if anyone
had considered whether or not i
wanted to live at that point.
-carrie arnold.

some one find me a
little boat with a glass
bottom, and i,ll go
hunting for sea pens.
find me a sea pen and i
will write love letters
to all of the crabs.
find me a seaweed dress
and i'll marry all the
drift wood.

sea birds
be damned.

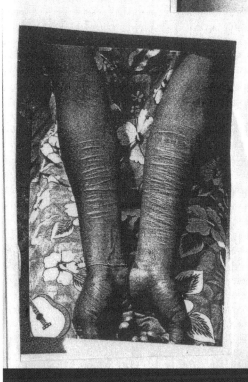

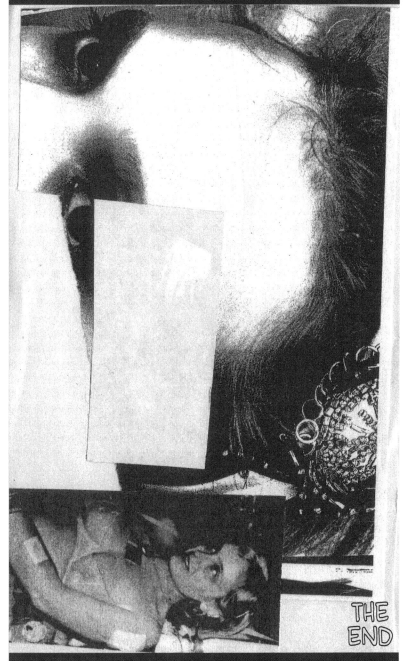

THE
END

About the author:

Neely Bat Chestnut has traveled the country (and other countries) teaching zine workshops. In her spare times she scouts out deals on old pyrex at rummage sales with her friend Rebecca, sings in a metal band, Ire Adrift, and sews clothes for her blythe dolls. She repaints the rooms in her house everytime she grows tired of a colour and has a knack for finding fabulous old wool coats and cat eye glasses. She shares her home with two rabbits, a pellet stove, and an extensive Beatrix Potter collection.

Made in the USA
Charleston, SC
30 December 2012